B. .MING LOCAL CHURCH

BECOMING LOCAL CHURCH

Historical, Theological and Missiological Essays

JAMES H. KROEGER

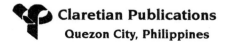
Claretian Publications
Quezon City, Philippines

BECOMING LOCAL CHURCH:
Historical, Theological and Missiological Essays

Copyright © 2003 by: **James H. Kroeger**

Published 2003 by:
Claretian Publications, Inc.
U.P.P.O. Box 4 Diliman, 1101 Quezon City, Philippines
Tel.: 921-3984 • FAX: 921-6205
E-mail: claret@cnl.net • Website: http://www.bible.claret.org

Claretian Publications is a pastoral endeavor of the Claretian Missionaries in the Philippines. It aims to promote a renewed spirituality rooted in the process of total liberation and solidarity in response to the needs, challenges, and pastoral demands of the Church today.

Paintings on Cover:
"Evangelization of the Philippines" - Alfredo Juson
"Blessed Pedro Calungsod" - Alfredo Esquillo
"Saint Lorenzo Ruiz" - Chito Dajao, SDB

Photographs of Paintings: James H. Kroeger, M.M.

Library of Congress Cataloging-in-Publication Data

Kroeger, James H., 1945-
BECOMING LOCAL CHURCH:
Historical, Theological and Missiological Essays
p. x + 138   cm. 15.24 x 22.86
ISBN 971-501-966-8

1. Catholic Church—Asia. 2. Catholic Church—Bishops—Asia.
3. Catholic Church—Philippines. 4. Theology, Doctrinal.
I. Kroeger, James H., 1945- II. Title.

BX1746.K912 2003
262.7—dc21

CONTENTS

PREFACE

Local Church—a central theme in contemporary ecclesiology. *Local Church*—a decisive factor in the life and mission of a mature, authentic Christian community. *Local Church*—cornerstone of today's emerging, inculturated faith-communities in all the continents. *Local Church*—focal point of the evangelizing mission of the Church.

The foregoing assertions about the pivotal role of the local Church today are not mere hyperbole. They reflect the vision and experience of the worldwide Church. The Asian bishops (FABC), for example, consistently attest to the importance of local Church. They see that the "building up of the local Church [is] the present focus of the Church's mission in Asia." This task demands that "the local Churches in Asia must see themselves as responsible agents for the self-realization of the Church." In a word, the local Church is to be "the acting subject of mission."

Again, FABC documents boldly assert: "If the Asian Churches do not discover their own identity, they will have no future." This process calls "on the part of the Churches for originality, creativity and inventiveness, for boldness and courage." In short, the Churches of Asia must discover "a new way of being Church"! Local Churches—succinctly stated— "Their time has come for Asia"!

This book, a collection of five scholarly essays, presents various dimensions of the thematic of local Church. The first essay is a brief historical and contemporary overview of one local Church, that of the Philippines; it shows that being local Church is always a concrete, incarnated, experiential phenomenon. The second essay captures the powerful, inspiring, and programmatic FABC vision of becoming a vibrant local Church.

Three additional essays address aspects of an emerging local Church: commitment to integral evangelization, interreligious dialogue, and mission and conversion in a paschal perspective. While these three pieces are primarily developed around a central theme, their relationship to the local Church is always briefly explored.

These five essays have been previously published in theological or missiological journals. The author, however, has thoroughly revised and updated each piece. The selected bibliographies attached to each essay are not limited only to the paper itself; they are designed, using 40-50 authors and sources, to be a current panorama of the best literature on the specific subject area under discussion.

The reader will most certainly detect a partial "Asian bias" in these essays and bibliographies. This flows from the author's conviction that some of the best theological reflection and pastoral-missiological application on the theme of local Church has emerged in Asia and through the experience of the Churches of the FABC region. And, since all theology and experience is ultimately contextual, these essays will mirror some of the author's more than three decades of missionary service in both the Philippines and Bangladesh. The author has been privileged to journey with God's holy people of these two local Churches and to participate in discerning "what the Spirit is saying to / through the Churches in Asia" (cf. Rev. 2:7). This experience has definitely been an inspiring and invigorating discovery of the pathways of the Spirit in the local Churches of Asia.

Pentecost 2003

James H. Kroeger, M.M.
Loyola School of Theology
Manila, Philippines

AN EMERGING LOCAL CHURCH

The Philippine Experience

The Roman Catholic Church in the Philippines is a major actor in this Southeast Asian island nation as well as within the wider Asian Church and in the Universal Church. Statistics at the beginning of the third millennium show 85% of Filipinos as Catholics (64.5 million of a total population of 75.8 million); this fact makes the Philippines the world's third largest local Church (after Brazil and Mexico). Of Asia's 105 million Catholics over 60% are Filipinos. These brief, yet significant, facts invite deeper exploration of the multi-faceted Philippine Church.

BACKGROUND. The Philippine archipelago is composed of 7,107 islands and islets, of which the largest are Luzon in the north and Mindanao in the south. In central Philippines are several medium-sized islands known as the Visayan Islands. Stretching from the southwestern tip of Mindanao toward Borneo is a chain of small islands collectively known as the Sulu Archipelago. The population of southwestern Mindanao and Sulu is predominantly Muslim.

There is evidence of human settlements in the islands as early as 20,000 BC. The small black people, called Negritos by the Spaniards, were the first to arrive. Later they were driven into the mountainous interior when immigrants belonging to the brown-skinned Malay race reached the islands. Today one finds various hill tribes such as the Aetas and Ifugao of Luzon and the Mansakas, Mandayas, and Bukidnon of Mindanao; many of these peoples still practice their traditional religions. Malay Filipinos occupy the lowlands, constitute the majority of the population, and have become Christian. They form several linguistic groups of which the Bisaya, Tagalog, Ilokano, Pampango, and Bikol are most numerous.

ARRIVAL OF SPANIARDS. In March 1521 Ferdinand Magellan arrived in search of spices and converts for Charles I (Emperor Charles V); it was his son Prince Philip, later King Philip II, whose name was bestowed on the islands by Villalobos in 1542. Lapulapu, a native chieftain of Cebu, resisted Magellan's claim of Spanish sovereignty and he was mortally wounded by Lapulapu's spear thrust. In 1565 Miguel Lopez de Legazpi established the first permanent Spanish settlement in Cebu. In 1571 Legazpi moved his headquarters to Manila, making it the capital of the colony. By the end of the century, most of the lowlands were under Spanish rule, except for some southern islands which remained Muslim.

Islam had been introduced in the late fourteenth or early fifteenth century. It gradually exercised a strong influence and helped develop a type of sophisticated political organization, semifeudal and predatory, in Mindanao and Sulu and initially in Manila. When the Spaniards encountered Muslims in the Philippines their hostile attitudes based on Muslim-Christian encounters in Europe (the struggle for independence from Moorish rule in the Iberian

Peninsula) colored their outlook and relations; these very negative attitudes were also transmitted to non-Muslim Filipinos.

SYSTEMATIC CHRISTIANIZATION. An organized program of evangelization of the Philippines was begun in 1565 by the Augustinians who accompanied Legazpi's expedition. They were followed by Franciscans (1578), Jesuits (1581), Dominicans (1587), and Augustinian Recollects (1606) from both Spain and Mexico. Manila became a bishopric in 1579 and an archbishopric in 1595.

The Spanish system of the *Patronato Real*, or royal patronage of the Church in the Indies, facilitated the implementation of the evangelization program. Under this arrangement, the Spanish crown gave financial support and protection to the Church in the Philippines while exercising a large measure of control over its activities. Missionaries traveled to the Philippines in the king's ships. While engaged in mission work, they were entitled to a stipend drawn from either the colonial government directly or from the right to tribute in certain territories (*encomiendas*) into which the country was initially divided. The *encomienda* system was gradually abandoned during the seventeenth century after widespread criticism of extortion and other abuses.

On the other hand, the appointment of missionaries to a parish or mission station was subject to the approval of the governor as vice-patron. In fact, it was Philip II himself who determined that each missionary group should have its own section of the country for evangelization purposes. Under this system the Church in turn exerted great influence on government policy. The early missionaries often sought to protect the natives from the abuses of the conquistadors and *encomenderos*; they had a vigorous leader in Fray Domingo de Salazar, OP, the first bishop of the Philippines. The synod that he summoned in 1582 clarified many difficult problems regarding the conquest, settlement, and administration of the country in accordance with Christian ideals and principles of justice.

The Philippine Church of the sixteenth century certainly took sides, and it was not with the rich and powerful nor with their fellow Spaniards, but with those who were oppressed and victims of injustice. Church historian Schumacher notes: "Skeptics have often questioned the reality of the rapid conversion of sixteenth-century Filipinos. If one wishes the answer, it is to be found right here, that the Church as a whole took the side of the poor and the oppressed, whether the oppressors were Spaniards or Filipino *principales*."

MISSION METHODS. The Spanish missionaries in the Philippines employed a variety of approaches to evangelization. The scattered clan villages were gathered together into larger communities (*pueblos, cabeceras*); often this implied radical lifestyle changes and hence could only be accomplished with difficulty and very gradually. Instruction was given in native languages, as few Filipinos outside the Intramuros area of Manila were ever able to read, write, or speak Spanish with any proficiency. In most missions primary schools supplied the new Christian communities with catechists and local officials. Religion was made to permeate society by substituting splendid liturgical and paraliturgical observances (*fiestas*, processions, novenas) for the traditional rites and festivals; many pious associations of prayer and charity were formed and promoted.

EDUCATION AND SOCIAL SERVICES. These tasks were almost exclusively the concern of the Church during the entire period of Spanish rule. Before the end of the sixteenth century, Manila had three hospitals, one for Spaniards, another for natives, and a third for the Chinese. The first two were conducted by Franciscans, the third by the Dominicans. Later (1611) the Hospitallers of Saint John of God came to make hospital work their special field of activity. In 1595 the Jesuits opened a grammar school for Spanish boys that later developed into the University of San Ignacio and had attached to it the residential college of San José, founded in 1601 and today the San José Seminary.

The year 1611 saw the beginnings of the Dominican University of Santo Tomás, which continues today as a vibrant educational center. In 1640 the Dominicans also took charge of the College of San Juan de Letrán, started about a decade earlier by a zealous layman for the education of orphans. Various religious communities of women established themselves in Manila in the seventeenth and eighteenth centuries; frequently, they undertook the education of girls. Among these sisterhoods, that begun by Ignacia del Espírito Santo, a Chinese *mestiza*, in 1684 and today known as the Religious of the Virgin Mary (RVM), deserves special mention as the first locally founded religious institute specifically for indigenous women.

FINANCIAL SUPPORT. The considerable funds required for the support of these schools, hospitals, and charitable works came from pious donations and legacies, called *obras pías*; they were often invested in the galleon trade or in large agricultural estates, the so-called friar lands. These operations often tainted the Church as being involved with commercialism. At the same time, the friar lands were leased to tenant cultivators for development and administration, an arrangement that led to frequent conflicts of interest and a deepening resentment of the Church as landlord. This background must be borne in mind for a balanced understanding of the anticlerical reaction that developed in the latter nineteenth century among a people deeply and sincerely Catholic.

NATIVE CLERGY. Catholicism had taken permanent root in the Philippines as the religion of the people by the eighteenth century, if not earlier. However, it had one serious weakness: the retarded development of the native clergy. The unsatisfactory results of early experiments in Latin America had made the Spanish missionaries in the Philippines extremely cautious in admitting native candidates to the priesthood. Apparently, only in the late seventeenth century were native Filipinos ordained. A proposal of Gianbattista Sidotti, a member of Cardinal Charles de Tournon's entourage, to erect a regional seminary in Manila for the whole of East Asia was sharply rejected by the crown (1712).

Bishops became increasingly eager for a diocesan clergy completely under their jurisdiction when conflicts over parish appointments continued— conflicts between the bishops and the religious orders on the one hand, and the bishops and the government on the other. Since very few secular priests came to the Philippines from Spain, this meant ordaining large numbers of natives. Archbishop Sancho de Santa Justa y Rufina of Manila (1767-1787) threatened to take away their parishes from the religious who refused to submit to episcopal visitation; he also ordained natives even when they lacked the necessary aptitude and training.

The results proved disastrous, confirming the prevailing opinion that natives, even if admitted to the priesthood, were incapable of assuming its full responsibilities. Some improvement in formation and an increase in vocations occurred after the arrival of the Vincentians (1862), who took charge of diocesan seminaries. Even so, the departure of a large proportion of Spanish clergy after the transfer of sovereignty from Spain to the United States (1898) left over 700 parishes vacant.

RELIGIOUS CLERGY. The privileges of the *Patronato Real* conferred by the Holy See on the Spanish crown were a mixed blessing; they promoted constructive collaboration between the Church and the colonial government, but also led to friction. The focus of difficulty was the religious parish priest and the extent to which he was subject to episcopal visitation and control. The conflict gave rise to series of crises that began as early as the administration of Bishop Salazar (1581-1594). In 1744 the Holy See ruled that religious parish priests were subject to the jurisdiction of the ordinary in all matters pertaining to their parish duties (*in officio officiando*) and to their religious superiors in their personal conduct.

With the advent of the revolutionary era in Europe and the loss of Spain's American colonies, the terms of the problem in the Philippines changed. It became widely believed in official circles that the presence of the religious in the parishes was a political necessity, not so much because they were religious as because they were Spaniards and could be relied upon to keep the population loyal. This seems to have been the thinking behind the royal decree of 1862 transferring the Mindanao missions from the Augustinian Recollects to the newly returned Jesuits (they had been expelled in 1768) and giving the former an equivalent number of parishes in Manila and Cavite, which were consequently taken away from the native clergy. The result was mounting disaffection among the native priests thus deprived or threatened with removal. Naturally, the Filipino priests assailed the government policy; among their active leaders and spokesmen were Fathers Gómez, Burgos, and Zamora, who were executed by the government for alleged complicity in a mutiny of native garrison troops in Cavite (1872).

The deaths of these Filipino priests gave a powerful impetus to the emergence of Filipino nationalism by sensitizing Filipinos to injustices by the Spanish colonial government. The movement began as an initiative for colonial reforms led by Dr. José Rizal (1862-1896); after Rizal's arrest and execution for treason, it developed into a separatist movement. The ensuing revolution (1896-1898), which was markedly anti-friar, though usually not anticlerical or anti-Catholic, was cut short by the intervention of the United States, which demanded cession of the Philippines at the conclusion of the Spanish-American War.

SEPARATION OF CHURCH AND STATE. The change of sovereignty ended the *Patronato* system. The United States' policy of Church-State separation was extended to the Philippines, but interpreted in a manner much less favorable to the Church. Thus, a system of nonsectarian public education was established that failed to take into account that the overwhelming majority of Filipinos were Catholics. In addition, there was the strong influence of hundreds of American public-school teachers, most of whom were Protestants. They were popularly known as the Thomasites; a group of 540 arrived in 1901 aboard the *U.S.S. Thomas* and many others followed. The professed neutralism in religious matters of the state university, founded in 1911, was copied by other privately founded nonsectarian universities, resulting in the undermining of religious belief among the educated class.

SCHISM. One consequence of the revolutionary upheaval was the formation by Gregorio Aglipay, a Filipino secular priest, of a schismatic church along nationalist lines, the Philippine Independent Church or *Iglesia Filipina Independiente* (1902). Initially it drew a considerable following; however, it soon broke up into factions, some of which rapidly deserted Catholicism in doctrine as well as in discipline. The Supreme Court (1906-1907) also restored to the Catholic Church much of the property that had been taken over by the Aglipayans. The largest Trinitarian faction was received into full communion by the Protestant Episcopal Church (United States), established in the Philippines since the beginning of the century.

PROTESTANT MISSIONS. Protestant denominations sent mission personnel to the Philippines almost as soon as the transfer of sovereignty was effected. In 1901 Presbyterian, Baptist, Methodist, and United Brethren groups, along with societies such as the Christian Missionary Alliance, the YMCA, and the American Bible Society, formed an Evangelical Union to coordinate their activities. A denomination of local origin with an evangelical orientation, the *Iglesia ni Cristo*, was founded in 1914.

CHURCH RESPONSE. The normal life of the Catholic Church suffered disastrously during the years following 1898; in several respects it would be decades before a condition approximating "normalcy" would again be reached. From 1898 to 1900 there were almost no resident bishops; diocesan priests remained in very short supply and some had defected to the Aglipayans; seminaries were closed in 1898 and did not reopen until 1904. From 1898 to 1903 the total number of friars decreased over 75% from 1,013 to 246. In a word, the Church was in chaos.

The true beginnings of the reorganization of the Church began with the persistent efforts of Monsignor Guidi through his negotiations with the American government and the Filipino clergy. Leo XIII, in his apostolic letter *Quae mari sinico* (1902) reorganized the hierarchy, created four new dioceses, and strongly recommended to the Philippine hierarchy the formation of a native clergy. The first official Provincial Council of Manila was convened in 1907 with the goals of reviving the faith of the Filipinos, restoring the local Church, and inspiring in the clergy a spirit of apostolic zeal.

Meanwhile, the severe shortage of priests and religious was met in part by new, non-Spanish missionary congregations of women and men from Europe, Australia, and America. For example, male missionary societies that responded to the pressing needs in the 1905-1941 period are: Irish Redemptorists (1905), Mill Hill Missionaries (1906), Scheut-CICM (1907), Sacred Heart Missionaries and Divine Word Society (1908), LaSalle Brothers (1911), Oblates of Saint Joseph (1915), Maryknoll Missioners (1926), Columban Missioners (1929), Society of Saint Paul (1935), Quebec-PME Society (1937), and Oblates-OMI (1939). Many dedicated female religious came as missionaries to the Philippines, often working in partnership with the societies just mentioned.

By the mid-1920s, the situation was taking a turn for the better; some significant factors in the survival and resurgence of the Church were: the revitalization of Catholic education, growth of Filipino diocesan and religious vocations, a more educated laity, Church involvement in social questions and the labor movement, and the involvement of Catholics in national life. The celebration of the XXXIII International Eucharistic Congress in Manila (1937) focused the attention of the Christian world on the Philippines and deeply inspired thousands of Filipino Catholics.

SECOND WORLD WAR. Japanese forces invaded in December 1941. Allied forces under General MacArthur returned in 1944, but severe fighting continued until the Japanese surrender in August 1945. Manuel Roxas became president of the second independent Republic of the Philippines on July 4, 1946. The war inflicted heavy damage; 257 priests and religious lost their lives, and losses in ecclesiastical property and equipment were estimated at **P**250 million (U.S.$ 125 million). Priests, brothers, sisters, and dedicated Catholic women and men exhibited great faith and heroism during the war; many suffered imprisonment.

ORGANIZATION OF PHILIPPINE BISHOPS. The origins of what is known today as the Catholic Bishops' Conference of the Philippines (CBCP) can be traced back to February 1945 when Apostolic Delegate William Piani, even as the war was still raging, appointed John Hurley, SJ to take charge of relief work and created the Catholic Welfare Organization (CWO). As the very name indicates, the primary purpose of the CWO was to assist in alleviating the immediate suffering and destruction brought on by the war. On July 17, 1945 all the bishops met in Manila for their first meeting after the Japanese Occupation; they requested that the CWO become the official organization of the Hierarchy of the Philippines. In subsequent years, the CWO continued to be largely engaged in relief services and the rehabilitation of Church institutions; it also became the vehicle through which the interests and values of the Church were protected and furthered.

The 1945-1965 period in the life of the local Church in the Philippines is characterized by: quite rapid recovery from the ravages of war, greatly expanded school system at upper levels, involvement of Catholics (laity, sisters, clergy) in social action, and growing Filipinization of Church structures and administration. The First Plenary Council of the Philippines (1953) focused on the "preservation, enrichment, and propagation of Catholic life" and offered Church resources "to renew the social order." The Church became involved in Catholic Action programs with farmers (FFF) and workers (FFW). Guidance from the hierarchy continued; from 1945-1965 the CWO issued 39 joint pastoral letters and statements on a variety of subjects relevant to Church and civil society. The Philippine bishops sponsored a Marian Congress in Manila (1954) and inaugurated the Pontificio Collegio-Seminario Filippino in Rome (1961). The period saw renewal programs introduced; the Christian Family Movement (CFM) came to the Philippines in the 1950s; the *Cursillos de Cristianidad* introduced in 1963 (and the evangelization seminars for various Church sectorial groups they inspired) ignited a renewed fervor of lay involvement in the Church.

1965: A PIVOTAL YEAR. In mid-year, the nation observed a six-day renewal-celebration of the quadricentennial of evangelization in the Philippines

(1565-1965). The bishops established the Mission Society of the Philippines, signifying Filipinos' commitment to spread the gift of faith they had received to other lands. Two more events would prove to shape significantly the experience and mission of this local Church. The first was the election of Ferdinand Marcos as president of the Philippines; the second was the conclusion of the Second Vatican Council.

AUTHORITARIAN RULE. The Philippine constitution, modeled on that of the United States, established a democratic form of government. Ferdinand E. Marcos, first elected president in 1965, declared martial law in 1972 and imposed a form of "constitutional authoritarianism." The martial law period posed new, challenging questions for the Church and nation. Among the more pernicious effects of the two-decade Marcos era (1965-1986) were increased militarization, insurgency, the absence of juridical procedures, the destruction of democratic processes, economic decline, and pervasive fear. The end result, in the words of a Filipino social scientist, was to place the country "on the trembling edge of a social volcano."

This period proved a time of testing and growth for the local Church. Prophetic stances were often met by military abuse, imprisonment and torture, and even deportation for foreign missionaries. The Church evolved a position of "critical collaboration," cooperating with the regime on programs beneficial to the populace while criticizing government actions judged harmful.

An important 1977 pastoral letter, *The Bond of Love in Proclaiming the Good News*, addressed many social problems as well as the divisions within the Church

created by various positions taken vis-à-vis martial law
(e.g. the absence of a clear stance and the long-delayed
response on the part of most members of the hierarchy;
the infiltration of Church structures and institutions
by left-leaning priests and religious). The pastoral
letter sought to enunciate a clear, holistic vision to
guide the Church's mission of integral evangelization:

> This is EVANGELIZATION: the proclamation,
> above all, of SALVATION from sin; the liberation from
> everything oppressive to man; the DEVELOPMENT
> of man in all his dimensions, personal and
> communitarian; and ultimately, the RENEWAL OF
> SOCIETY in all its strata through the interplay of the
> GOSPEL TRUTHS and man's concrete TOTAL LIFE....
> THIS IS OUR TASK. THIS IS OUR MISSION.

President Marcos announced the lifting of martial
law on January 17, 1981. It was carefully timed—three
days before the inauguration of United States
President Ronald Regan, and exactly one month before
Pope John Paul II's scheduled visit to the Philippines.
In view of the broad range of authoritarian controls
retained by Marcos, the lifting of martial law was
recognized by the Filipino people as a purely cosmetic
gesture. The papal visit brought two clear messages
to Filipinos: a need for dynamic faith in their lives
and an emphasis on justice and peace. Specifically,
John Paul II told the president and government leaders:
"Even in exceptional situations that may at times arise,
one can never justify any violation of the fundamental
dignity of the human person or of the basic rights that
safeguard this dignity."

The assassination of Benigno Aquino on August
21, 1983 ushered in a period of national mourning and
a widespread clamor for justice and truth. In this
highly charged atmosphere the local Church's response

was crucial. Jaime Cardinal Sin, Archbishop of Manila since 1974, cautioned Filipinos: "If we allow his death to fan the flames of violence and division, then he will have died in vain."

Events moved rapidly in the ensuing years. Filipino consciousness had been awakened; Philippine society had been galvanized. The Church did not remain on the sidelines during this national crisis. In the volatile context that followed the elections of 1986, the Catholic bishops issued a statement declaring that fraud provides no moral legitimacy for any regime. If citizens agreed that the election had been "stolen," they should oblige the regime to respect their will. The bishops added: "But we insist: Our acting must always be according to the Gospel of Christ, that is, in a peaceful, non-violent way."

PEOPLE POWER ONE. An analysis of the story of the "bloodless revolution" of February 1986 and the roles played by Church people and Cardinal Sin is instructive. The overthrow of the Marcos regime was "a victory of *moral* values over the sheer physical force on which he had relied" [J. Carroll]. It signaled people's determination not to shed Filipino blood. The revolution was a "movement for active non-violence which was promoted by Church-related groups" [*ibid.*]. In addition, "the February Revolution was a *political* event, not a social revolution" [*ibid.*]. Basic social issues of wealth and power that plagued the nation for generations remained. Many Filipinos still found themselves outside the mainstream of national social, political, and economic life.

AQUINO PRESIDENCY. Corazon C. Aquino, catapulted into office with little experience, served as Philippine president from 1986-1992. Aquino's main contribution was the reestablishment of a democratically functioning government. She began by enacting a temporary "freedom constitution." In May 1986, Aquino appointed a constitutional commission (including Church people) and asked that a new document be produced within three months. This constitution was ratified overwhelmingly by a national referendum in 1987.

Difficult issues faced Aquino: a bankrupt economy, communist insurgents, the status of the United States military bases, coup plotters, natural disasters, a burgeoning population, Islamic separatists, the foreign debt, agrarian reform—the list appeared endless. Yet, she guided the Filipino people to free and fair elections in May 1992 and the orderly transfer of power to President Fidel Ramos (1992-1998), the first Protestant president of the Philippines.

ASSESSING THE SOCIAL SITUATION. The Marcos years (1965-1986) further accentuated the mass poverty that had long been and continues to be the most tragic aspect of Filipino life. Per capita income in 2000 was estimated at $1,046 per year; nearly 50% of Filipinos were living below the poverty line. The foreign debt in 2000 was $52.4 billion; in the Marcos years alone it moved from a manageable $599 million to $26 billion. Servicing the domestic and foreign debt absorbs an average of 40% of the government budget. In 2000 the unemployment rate was 11.8% and underemployment stood at 22%. Filipinos are found in 193 countries of the world; overseas foreign workers are 2.96 million; undocumented personnel are 1.91 million; there are 2.33 million permanent residents overseas. The total number of Filipinos overseas is 7.2 million—fully 10% of the total population. Locally, graft and corruption remain prevalent—even endemic; environmental degradation continues; the infant mortality rate is high. In stark contrast to the prevalent poverty, there are pockets of great luxury, underlining the gross inequity of income distribution.

In the political system, power, like wealth, is concentrated in the hands of a few influential politicians, business and military people. There appears to be a self-perpetuating social system and political culture. Politicians, for the most part, have not introduced truly transformative social programs into their platforms.

In contemporary Philippines, diverse ideologies, with varying political visions and programs, all promise a better life for the Filipino. There are both non-violent and armed or revolutionary positions. The left is usually identified with the Communist Party of the Philippines (CPP), its militant New People's Army (NPA), and the National Democratic Front (NDF), which it dominates. The revolutionary left's protracted struggle has caused destruction; a small group of Church workers continues to promote this Marxist-Leninist-Maoist ideology. In southern Philippines, two Islamic political groups continue to be serious threats to peace.

The Philippine local Church, following the lead of Vatican II, seeks to involve itself with the lives and struggles of Filipinos, their "joys, hopes, griefs, and anxieties" (cf. GS 1). Recently, Church leaders wrote: "Such are the challenges that the Church has to face in its evangelizing and liberating mission. We have to bring our considerable resources as people of God to bear upon these problems."

The political fortunes of the Filipino people and the consequent social and economic ramifications have helped shape the very identity and perspectives of the local Church. In a word, the *context* has shaped the believing community and has significantly influenced the *content* of its program of evangelization; all these elements are necessary ingredients for a full appreciation of the vibrant Catholicism present in the Philippines today.

IMPLEMENTATION OF VATICAN II. The Second Vatican Council promoted a major ecclesiological paradigm shift, entailing changes in theologies, values, and orientations. Received by the local Church of the Philippines, it prompted the Filipino bishops to launch a New Evangelization; the social apostolate was among its emphases. Early efforts centered on the formation and support of unions and cooperatives for farmers, laborers, and fishermen. The bishops issued several pastoral letters on social action, justice and development. They sponsored a National Rural Development Congress in 1967, the slogan of which, "The Church Goes to the Barrios," became axiomatic for the Church's commitment to development and social justice. The bishops established and funded the National Secretariat for Social Action, Justice, and Peace (NASSA) as their means of coordinating the social justice apostolate. The influential Mindanao-Sulu Pastoral Conference (MSPC) was established in 1971.

In the late 1960s and early 1970s, the Church's vision of human development as integral to evangelization expanded from a concern for social change to include the need for structural change. It became clear that efforts that had improved the conditions of the farming and working classes could not be sustained without corresponding political leverage. Church involvement in broader social, political, and economic questions became imperative.

Vatican II ecclesiology has taken root in the Philippine Church. Growth has often been difficult and uncertain; it has required deep faith to discern and follow the Spirit's promptings in the midst of challenging historical circumstances and social conditions. Yet, this journey has resulted in a mature, vibrant local Church. The presence of strong Base Christian Communities (BECs) provides grass roots structures for spiritual, catechetical, ministerial, and social growth. Important strengths are present in this Church: the inductive and experimental approach of theology; its inculturated social teaching; its spirituality of human development; its renewed ecclesiology/missiology; its concrete service to many Filipinos facing diverse dehumanizing social ills; its engagement in social issues in a non-partisan but active manner; its efforts to promote and practice non-violent approaches to socio-political crises; its commitment to create structures of participation in Church and society. The Church also has its recent witnesses—and martyrs: Bishop Benjamin de Jesus, OMI (February 4, 1997), Father Rhoel Gallardo, CMF (May 3, 2000), and Father Benjamin Inocencio, OMI (December 28, 2000).

The Philippine bishops have continued, with moderate effectivity, to use pastoral letters to communicate their holistic vision of the Church's evangelizing mission. In the post-Vatican II era, the CBCP (Catholic Bishops' Conference of the Philippines, canonically constituted in 1967) has issued 125+ pastoral letters and statements (1965-2000). Approximately two-thirds of these documents address social, political, and economic matters; Bishop Claver notes that they have generally proven to be quite accurate barometers of Philippine life. This effective tool of evangelization has promoted a basic Christian "faith-realism" and continually needs to be actualized within viable Christian communities.

The local Church today retains moral authority and credibility in Philippine society; its witness to justice and solidarity with the poor, marginalized, and oppressed has established a reservoir of good will and credibility. Yet, as a living organism, she has clear limitations. There were unfortunate divisions in Church leadership, particularly in the mid-1970s; this resulted in missed pastoral opportunities and negative influences on the broader Church membership. Some bishops were hesitant to engage in human development programs and prophetic evangelization— especially during the early years of martial law. Although indigenous clergy and religious continue to increase, that growth rate is below the percentage of population increase; the priest-Catholic ratio is one of the lowest in the world. There is also a glaring inequitable distribution of apostolic personnel within the country; concentrations are usually found in urban areas.

CATECHESIS AND EDUCATION. Given the large and rapidly expanding population of the Philippines (43 million in 1975 to 75.8 million in 2000), catechesis for Catholics remains a basic area of Church renewal. The catechetical ministry has shown considerable growth in vision, publications, institutes, and personnel. The Episcopal Commission on Catechesis and Catholic Education (ECCCE) has published several works and sponsored a variety of national workshops and congresses. Significant publications include: *The Shape of Religious Education in the Philippines* (1979), *National Catechetical Directory for the Philippines* (1982-1985), *Filipino Family Growing in the Faith* (1983), *The Catechists' Basic Formation Program* (1992), *Catholic Faith Catechism* (1989-1993), *Catechism for Filipino Catholics*

(1997) and its Tagalog translation *Katesismo para sa mga Pilipinong Katoliko* (2000). ECCCE publishes a quarterly catechetical review, *Docete*, which has raised interest in and the quality level of catechesis throughout the country.

Significant catechetical congresses have been sponsored by ECCCE in the 1990s, beginning with the celebration of the National Catechetical Year (1990). Diocesan catechetical institutes have been established in major cities (e.g. Bacolod, Cebu, Davao, Iloilo. Manila, Naga, Vigan, etc.). Other national centers which prepare women and men for their vocation as catechists (e.g. Mother of Life Center, Manila) continue their decades of service. The Philippine Constitution affords opportunities for religious education in public schools; this critical area of the catechetical ministry is limited by inadequate numbers of suitably formed catechists. The local Church is also quite unprepared to meet the new emphasis in ongoing and adult catechesis.

The Philippine Church has made a major commitment to formal education. It operates hundreds of high schools and grade schools as well as over 300 colleges and universities. The Catholic Educational Association of the Philippines (CEAP), founded in 1941, continues to represent the interests of Catholic educational institutions and promote religious instruction. Similar activities are the focus of the Association of Catholic Universities of the Philippines (ACUP), established in 1973.

A unique and successful form of religious education and renewal has evolved in the Philippine Church with the holding of large national congresses, dedicated to particular themes. Coming from all ecclesiastical circumscriptions, the delegates (often several thousand) are expected to become trainer-facilitators upon their return home; audio and video tapes as well as printed materials of the congresses are made available. This approach proved particularly effective in the years connected with the Great Jubilee 2000. A partial list includes the following: Marian Year (1985), Eucharistic Year (1987), Bible Year (1989), Catechetical Year (1990), World Youth Day (1995), Eucharistic Congress (1997), two Holy Spirit Congresses (1998), Congress on God the Father (1999), Congress on the Trinity (2000), and the National Mission Congress (2000). The local Church of the Philippines hosted the Fourth World Meeting of Families in January, 2003. Finally, the Church also supports liturgical centers, radio stations, publishing houses, hospitals, and social action centers throughout its 80+ dioceses.

LEARNING-TEACHING CHURCH. In 1995 the Bishops' Conference (CBCP) celebrated its fiftieth year since beginning in 1945 as the Catholic Welfare Organization (CWO). This became an opportunity to review and assess the CBCP's nature, structure, mission, and functions. The CBCP amended its constitution and by-laws; it established the new offices dedicated to media, legal matters, research, bioethics, women, and the Church's cultural heritage. The CBCP now has 33 departments, commissions, and offices to address the many concerns of this local Church. In addition, the bishops relaunched *The CBCP Monitor* in a new format, initiated a weekly radio program, and established the CBCP Website [http://www.cbcponline.org].

Responsive to the call for renewal in *Tertio Millennio Adveniente*, the CBCP issued a series of exhaustive and in-depth pastoral exhortations, designed to address vital aspects of Philippine life and Christianity. Each document began with a quite thorough and substantive analysis of the carefully chosen topics: Philippine Politics (1997), Philippine Economy (1998), Philippine Culture (1999), and Philippine Spirituality (2000). The bishops concluded the series with their document: "Missions" and the Church in the Philippines: A Pastoral Letter on the Church's Mission in the New Millennium (July 2000). The CBCP also sponsored the large National Mission Congress, which they saw as the "fitting culminating activity" of the Jubilee Year celebrations and the "first step as a Local Church into the Third Millennium."

ADDITIONAL MINISTRIES. Dialogue and peace-building with a variety of partners remain a continuous commitment of the Philippine Church. She strove to be an instrument of reconciliation during the Marcos years; along with the National Council of Churches in the Philippines, she made several overtures to various leftist and armed groups. In their 1990 pastoral letter, *Seek Peace, Pursue It*, the bishops laid out a ten-point "path to peace." The Church also engages in interfaith dialogue with indigenous and Muslim peoples; the Silsilah movement and the pivotal Bishops-Ulama Forum (1996+) have fostered Muslim-Christian harmony in Southern provinces. The annual "Mindanao Week of Peace" was begun in 1999.

The Philippines has an impressive growing body of "local theology," often emerging from local communities discerning the "signs of the times" under the Holy Spirit's lead. Recurrent themes emerge: evangelization and mission, prayer and spirituality, peace-making and reconciliation, dialogue with peoples, cultures, and religious traditions. Several important theological, pastoral, catechetical, and mission journals are published; representative journals are: *Boletin Ecclesiastico de Filipinas, East Asian Pastoral Review, Landas, Philippiniana Sacra, Religious Life Asia*, and *World Mission*. Prominent among Filipino theologians are: C. Arévalo, T. Bacani, F. Claver, A. Co, D. Huang, A. Lagdameo, L. Legaspi, L. Mercado, O. Quevedo, and L. Tagle.

A definite sign of a vibrant local Church is its mission outreach. In mid-2000 Catholic Filipino missionaries numbered 1,329 women and 206 men from 69 religious congregations serving in some 80 countries. The bishops established the Mission Society of the Philippines (1965). Maryknoll founded the Philippine Catholic Lay Mission (1977). Cardinal Sin established the San Lorenzo Mission Institute (1987), whose goal is serving the Chinese; its patron is San Lorenzo Ruiz, the first Filipino saint, canonized in 1987. Pedro Calungsod, beatified on March 5, 2000, inspired the successful National Mission Congress 2000.

CONTINUING RENEWAL AND COMMITMENT. A major local Church milestone was achieved in the 1991 month-long Second Plenary Council of the Philippines (PCP-II). After three years of intense preparation, a total of 504 participants (including 165 lay faithful) gathered for a comprehensive review and renewal of Christian life. The Council boldly challenged the local Church to be "a *Community of Disciples, a Church of the Poor,* committed to the mission of *renewed integral evangelization,* toward building up of a new *civilization of life and love* in this land." A systematic implementation scheme was elaborated in the National Pastoral Plan, *In the State of Mission: Towards a Renewed Integral Evangelization,* approved by the bishops on July 11, 1993.

Ten years later (January 2001) 369 delegates gathered for the National Pastoral Consultation on Church Renewal (NPCCR) and reflected on "how far we as a Church have fulfilled the grand vision and mission proposed by PCP-II and the National Pastoral Plan." The evaluation was both sober and hopeful: "The Church in the Philippines has, to our shame, ... remained unchanged in some respects; ... we, as Church, have to confess some responsibility for many of the continuing ills of Philippine society.... We rejoice, however, in the perseverance and increase of many movements of renewal; ... we hear anew God's call to renewal." NPCCR recommitted the Church to nine focused pastoral priorities for the first decade of the new millennium; they center on: faith, formation, laity, poor, family, community-building, clergy renewal, youth, ecumenism-dialogue, and *ad gentes* mission.

Providentially, the NPCCR, as originally scheduled, took place during the week immediately following the "People Power II" events (January 16-20, 2001) that removed Joseph Estrada from the Philippine presidency after only a little over two years of his six-year term; Gloria Macapagal-Arroyo became the fourteenth president and the second woman to hold the highest office in the land. There was muted euphoria; the local Church had played a significant role; the event was described as "the gift of national and moral renewal which God empowered the Filipinos to receive." The tasks ahead were clear: democratic institutions need strengthening; confidence in government awaits restoration; poverty beckons amelioration; the economy needs rebuilding. The Philippine Church's commitment to "renewed integral evangelization" took on new depths and urgency.

Recalling the words of Pope John Paul II in *Novo Millennio Ineunte* where he quoted Luke 5:4: *Duc in Altum* (Put out into the Deep), the NPCCR final statement asserts:

> The challenge for us, the Church in the Philippines, is to do the same. We are called to put out into the depths of Philippine life and society, to put out into the depths of our life as Church, to put out our nets into the unknown depths of the future. Like Peter, we know the frustration of having caught nothing. But like Peter, we know that the One who directs us is the Lord who has renewed all things by his life, death and resurrection. And so we dare to begin again in the task of renewal. May Mary, star of evangelization, be with us in our journey to the new creation we so deeply desire.

* * *

SELECTED BIBLIOGRAPHY

THE PHILIPPINE LOCAL CHURCH

Achutegui, P. de, ed. *The "Miracle" of the Philippine Revolution.* Manila: Loyola School of Theology, 1986.

Anderson, G., ed. *Studies in Philippine Church History.* Ithaca, New York: Cornell University Press, 1969.

Arévalo, C. **[A]** "Prenotes to the Contextualization of Theology." *Philippiniana Sacra* 14/40 (January-April, 1979): 15-35. **[B]** "After Vatican II: Theological Reflection in the Church in the Philippines 1965-1987." *Landas* 2/1 (January, 1988): 11-24. **[C]** "Filipino Theology." In *Dictionary of Mission,* ed. Karl

Müller et al., 161-167. Maryknoll, New York: Orbis Books, 1997 [Extensive Bibliography].

Bacani, T. **[A]** *The Church and Politics.* Quezon City, Philippines: Claretian Publications, 1987. **[B]** *Preparing Our Future: The Pope and the Filipino Youth.* Manila: Gift of God Publications, 1994. **[C]** "The Ecclesiology of the Catholic Bishops' Conference of the Philippines [CBCP]." In *Anamnesis,* ed. F. Claver and P. Quitorio, 185-204. Manila: CBCP, 1996.

Bautista, F. *Cardinal Sin and the Miracle of Asia.* Manila: Reyes Publishing, Inc., 1987.

Bernad, M. *The Christianization of the Philippines: Problems and Perspectives.* Manila: The Filipiniana Book Guild, 1972.

Bernier, P. and M. Gabriel, ed. *Journeying with the Spirit: A Commentary on* PCP-II. Quezon City, Philippines: Claretian Publications, 1993.

Carroll, J. *Forgiving or Forgetting? Churches and the Transition to Democracy in the Philippines.* Manila: Institute on Church and Social Issues, 1999.

CBCP (Catholic Bishops' Conference of the Philippines). **[A]** *Acts and Decrees of the Second Plenary Council of the Philippines.* Manila: CBCP Secretariat, 1992. **[B]** *In the State of Mission: Towards a Renewed Integral Evangelization* [National Pastoral Plan]. Manila: CBCP Secretariat, 1993. **[C]** *Catechism for Filipino Catholics* [Tagalog Translation: *Katesismo para sa mga Pilipinong Katoliko*]. Manila: CBCP/ECCCE and Word and Life Publications, 1997 [2000].

Chupungco, A. "Liturgical Renewal in the Philippines." *Philippinum* Silver Anniversary Issue (October, 1987): 66-76.

Clark, F. **[A]** *Mission and the Philippines: Past, Present, Future* (2d ed., rev.). Pasay City, Philippines: Paulines, 2000. **[B]** *Asian Saints* (2d ed., rev). Quezon City, Philippines: Claretian Publications, 2000.

Claver, F. **[A]** *The Stones Will Cry Out: Grassroots Pastorals.*
Maryknoll, New York: Orbis Books, 1978. **[B]** "Philippine
Church and 'People Power'." *The Month* 19/5 (May, 1986): 149-
155. **[C]** Claver, F. and P. Quitorio ed. *Anamnesis 1995.* Manila: CBCP Secretariat, 1996.

De la Costa, H. *The Jesuits in the Philippines,* 1581-1768.
Cambridge, Massachusetts: Harvard University Press, 1961.

Elwood, D. *Toward a Theology of People Power.* Quezon
City, Philippines: New Day Publishers, 1988.

Fabros, W. *The Church and its Social Involvement in the Philippines, 1930-1972.* Quezon City, Philippines: Ateneo de Manila University, 1988.

Fernandez, P. *History of the Church in the Philippines,* 1521-
1898. Manila: National Book Store, 1979.

Galvez, J. *The Pioneers: Filipino Lay Missionaries.* Pasay
City, Philippines: Paulines, 1998.

Giordano, P. *Awakening to Mission: The Philippine Catholic
Church 1965-1981.* Quezon City, Philippines: New Day Publishers, 1988.

Gomez, H. *The Moro Rebellion and the Search for Peace: A
Study on Christian-Muslim Relations in the Philippines.* Zamboanga
City, Philippines: Silsilah Publications, 2000.

Huang, D. "Emerging Global, Postmodern Culture in
the Philippines." *Landas* 13/1 (1999): 48-58.

Kalaw-Tirol, L., ed. *Duet for EDSA: Chronology of a Revolution.* Manila: Foundation for Worldwide People Power, Inc.,
1995.

Kasaysayan: The Story of the Filipino People I-X. Hong Kong:
Asia Publishing Company Limited, 1998.

Kroeger, J. **[A]** *The Philippine Church and Evangelization:
1965-1984.* Rome: Pontifical Gregorian University, 1985 [Ex-
tensive Bibliography]. **[B]** *Church Truly Alive: Journey to the Fili-*

pino Revolution. Davao City, Philippines: Mission Studies Institute, 1988. **[C]** *Telling God's Story: National Mission Congress 2000*. Quezon City, Philippines: Claretian Publications, 2001.

Kwantes, A., ed. *Chapters in Philippine Church History*. Manila: OMF Literature, Inc., 2001.

LaRousse, W. *Walking Together, Seeking Peace: The Local Church of Mindanao-Sulu Journeying in Dialogue with the Muslim Community (1965-2000)*. Quezon City, Philippines: Claretian Publications, 2001 [Extensive Bibliography].

Latorre, R., ed. *Church Renewal: Proceedings and Addresses of the National Pastoral Consultation on Church Renewal*. Manila: CBCP Secretariat, 2001.

Legaspi, L. "The Church in the Philippines since 1900." *Boletin Eclesiastico de Filipinas* 39/435 (1965): 339-352.

Mabutas, A. "Evangelization in the Philippines." *East Asian Pastoral Review* 25/4 (1988): 371-378.

O'Brien, N. **[A]** *Revolution from the Heart*. Maryknoll, New York: Orbis Books, 1991. **[B]** *Island of Tears, Island of Hope: Living the Gospel in a Revolutionary Situation*. Quezon City, Philippines: Claretian Publications, 1994.

Pilario, D. "The Craft of Contextual Theology: Towards a Methodological Conversation in the Philippine Context." *Chakana: Intercultural Forum of Theology and Philosophy* [Aachen] 1/1 (2003): 19-42.

Quevedo, O. "Social Teachings and Social Transformation in CBCP Thought (1945-1995)." In *Anamnesis*, ed. F. Claver and P. Quitorio, 3-102. Manila: CBCP, 1996.

Quitorio, P., ed. **[A]** *Pastoral Letters: 1945-1995*. Manila: CBCP Secretariat, 1996. **[B]** *On the Threshold of the Next Millennium*. Manila: CBCP Publications, 1999.

Rosales, G. **[A]** "To Be the Subject of Mission: A Report on the International Mission Congress, Manila,

December 2-7, 1979." *Worldmission* [USA] 32/1 (Spring, 1981): 22-29. **[B]** ed. *"To Give Shining Witness"—The Church and Christians in the Philippines and "Mission" in the Eighties.* Manila: Pontifical Mission Aid Societies of the Philippines, 1981.

Santos, R. "Pontificio Collegio Filippino, 1961-2001." *Philippinum* 1/1 (2001): 178-252.

Sarmiento, J. ed. *Church, Politics and Transformation: Essays by Father Luis G. Hechanova, CSsR.* Quezon City, Philippines: Claretian Publications, 2002.

Schumacher, J. **[A]** *Revolutionary Clergy: The Filipino Clergy and the Nationalist Movement, 1850-1903.* Quezon City, Philippines: Ateneo de Manila University Press, 1981. **[B]** "Has the Philippine Church Been on the Side of the Poor?" *Life Forum* 16/3-4 (1984): 13-20. **[C]** *Readings in Philippine Church History* (2d ed. rev.). Quezon City, Philippines: Loyola School of Theology, 1987. **[D]** "Historical Errors." *Landas* 17/1 (2003): 119-122.

Sin, J. **[A]** "The Church in the Philippines: Twenty-seven Years after Vatican II." *Philippinum* Silver Anniversary Issue (October, 1987): 18-26. **[B]** "The Spirit of EDSA Dos." CBCP *Monitor* 7/2 (January 26, 2003): 12.

Tagle, L. *"It Is the Lord!"* Manila: Loyola School of Theology, 2003.

Yamsuan, P. and J. Garcia de la Cruz, ed. *John Paul II: We Love You* [1995 Papal Visit]. Manila: Asian Catholic Publishers, Inc., 1995.

Youngblood, R. *Marcos against the Church.* Ithaca, New York: Cornell University Press, 1990.

2

THEOLOGY OF LOCAL CHURCH
FABC Perspectives

Explore any major document that has emerged from the reflection of the Federation of Asian Bishops' Conferences (FABC) during its three-decade existence and you will find creative insights on the local Church in the Asian context. Historically, it was the 1970 Asian pastoral visit of Pope Paul VI that gave the impetus for the local Churches to begin formulating a vision of Church and mission adequate to the "new world being born" in Asia in the post-colonial period. They asked themselves: How would local faith-communities respond to the grace that was the Second Vatican Council? How would the Churches incarnate a decisive "turning to history" and a "turning to the Gospel" within history "for all the peoples of Asia"?

AN EMERGING THEOLOGY. Consistent, prolonged, pastoral and theological reflection on the Church and her mission of evangelization has enabled the FABC to articulate an overall vision that captures what "being Church in Asia today" truly means. The insights have grown out of a belief that the Spirit was speaking to the Churches. Without doubt, many creative FABC ecclesiological insights center on the meaning, theology, and lived experience of local Church.

FABC pastoral-theological reflection is decidedly inductive—emerging from life's concrete realities. Therefore, an ecclesiology with local Church as its focal point most adequately captures the hopes and aspirations of local peoples. As the community of Jesus' disciples in Asia, the Church consistently links her identity with Asia's peoples and their life situations. She seeks to be—in fact, not only in theory—the "Church of the poor" and the "Church of the young." She shares the vicissitudes of the "Church of silence" in several parts of Asia. Her pastoral priorities concern the displaced (refugees and migrants), women and the girl-child, youth, families, the poor, the followers of Asia's great religious traditions. She actively fosters increasing communion among Asia's local Churches in filial oneness with the See of Peter, which presides over the universal Church in love; she promotes authentic catholicity.

In a word, the theological thematic of *local Church* provides an appropriate, integrating center for the life of Asia's faith-communities. This fact helps explain why internationally some of the very best theological reflection on local Church has emerged in Asia and through the FABC. Telling the story of local Church in Asian / FABC theological reflection—with all its depth, richness, and inspiration—is the central focus of this modest essay. Methodologically, this presentation of FABC material on the local Church is unfolded chronologically; the format lends itself to greater clarity. In addition, quoting the FABC materials directly and extensively avoids diluting the freshness, creativity, and insightfulness of the original documents.

FABC I. The First FABC Plenary Assembly was held in Taipei, Taiwan in April 1974; it focused on the theme: "Evangelization in Modern Day Asia" (it was also a preparation for the Synod on Evangelization to be held in Rome later that same year). The Asian Churches through their bishops defined the central and most urgent mission duty incumbent upon them: "The primary focus of our task of evangelization then, at this time in our history, is the building up of a truly local church. For the local church is the realization and the enfleshment of the Body of Christ in a given people, a given place and time" (FABC I, 9-10).

"It is not a community in isolation from other communities of the Church one and catholic. Rather it seeks communion with all of them. With them it professes the one faith, shares the one Spirit and the one sacramental life. In a special way it rejoices in its communion and filial oneness with the See of Peter, which presides over the universal Church in love" (FABC I, 11).

"The local church is a church incarnate in a people, a church indigenous and inculturated. And this means concretely a church in continuous, humble and loving dialogue with the living traditions, the cultures, the religions—in brief, with all the life-realities of the people in whose midst it has sunk its roots deeply and whose history and life it gladly makes its own. It seeks to share in whatever truly belongs to that people: its meanings and its values, its aspirations, its thoughts and its language, its songs and its artistry. Even its frailties and failings it assumes, so that they too may be healed. For so did God's Son assume the totality of our fallen human condition (save only for sin) so that He might make it truly His own, and redeem it in His paschal mystery" (FABC I, 12).

ASIAN COLLOQUIUM ON MINISTRIES IN THE CHURCH. Three years later in 1977, during the Asian Colloquium on Ministries in the Church (ACMC) held in Hong Kong, the theme of local church received another impetus: "...the decisive new phenomenon for Christianity in Asia will be the emergence of genuine Christian communities in Asia—Asian in their way of thinking, praying, living, communicating their own Christ-experience to others. The consequences will be tremendous not only for the ministries the Asian Churches will have to perform but also for all aspects of their life. We should beware of seeing our future mission in categories that belong to the past, when the West shaped the Churches' history. If the Asian Churches do not discover their own identity, they will have no future" (ACMC 14).

"Each local Church is determined by her human context and lives in a dialectical relationship with the human society into which she is inserted as the Gospel leaven.... Each local Church, in order to be viable, needs to become fully responsible and must have the legitimate autonomy which her natural and harmonious growth demands" (ACMC 25).

"Asian Churches then must become truly Asian in all things. The principle of indigenization and inculturation is at the very root of their coming into their own. The ministry of Asian Churches, if it is to be authentic, must be relevant to Asian societies. This calls on the part of the Churches for originality, creativity and inventiveness, for boldness and courage" (ACMC 26).

"Since Christ's mission is universal, all local Churches are called to live in communion with each other. This bond of unity, visibly expressed in the college of bishops presided over by the Bishop of Rome, implies that the search of each Church for ministries adapted to her needs is subject to verification and testing by the other Churches. In this bond of union lies the guarantee of the true apostolicity and catholicity of each local Church" (ACMC 27).

FABC II. The Second FABC Plenary Assembly (Calcutta, India, 1978) was organized around the theme: "Prayer—The Life of the Church of Asia." The Bishops-delegate noted that an important motive for their assembly was "to deepen our knowledge of our local churches" (FABC II, 1), and they addressed "the tasks which the carrying-out of the mission of the Church in Asia demands: commitment to the upbuilding of Asian communities in the life of the Gospel, to inculturation of Christian faith and life, to the endeavor for total human development and authentic liberation of peoples in justice and love, to interreligious dialogue and to renewed missionary formation" (FABC II, 3).

INTERNATIONAL MISSION CONGRESS. The successful International (though predominantly Asian) Mission Congress (IMC) held in 1979 in Manila once again strongly affirmed the centrality of the local Church for a "new age of mission" in Asia.

"What is the newness of this 'new age of mission'? First, the realization in practice that 'mission' is no longer, and can no longer be, a one-way movement from the 'older churches' to the 'younger churches,' from the churches of the old Christendom to the churches in the colonial lands. Now—as Vatican II already affirmed with all clarity and force—every local church *is* and cannot be but missionary. Every local church is 'sent' by Christ and the Father to bring the Gospel to its surrounding milieu, and to bear it also into all the world. For every local church this is a *primary task*. Hence we are moving beyond both the vocabulary and the idea of 'sending churches' and 'receiving churches,' for as living communities of the one Church of Jesus Christ, every local church must be a sending church, and every local church (because it is not on earth ever a total realization of the Church) must also be a receiving church. Every local church is responsible for its mission, and co-responsible for the mission of all its sister-churches. Every local church, according to its possibilities, must share whatever its gifts are, for the needs of other churches, for mission throughout [hu]mankind, for the life of the world" (IMC 14).

"Once again, what is the newness of this 'new age of mission'? We believe that the Spirit of the Lord calls each people and each culture to its own fresh and creative response to the Gospel. Each local church has its own vocation in the one history of salvation, in the one Church of Christ. In each local church, each people's history, each people's culture, meanings and values, each people's traditions are taken up, not diminished nor destroyed, but celebrated and renewed, purified if need be, and fulfilled (as the Second Vatican Council teaches) in the life of the Spirit" (IMC 15).

Two workshop papers (V and VII) of the Manila Mission Congress spoke eloquently of the local Church. The participants of Workshop VII noted: "We recognize that the local church is the center and source of evangelization" (1). "Just as it is the responsibility of the Christian to work for the growth and development of the local church, in the same way he must become aware of his responsibility toward churches in other parts of the world" (9). This means: "Each local church is co-responsible with its sister churches everywhere, Rome being the foundation and center, for the building up of the kingdom of God throughout the world" (9).

The same document of Workshop VII affirms that "Missionaries from sister churches are not only living signs of the universality of the Church and the existence of co-responsibility, but because of their different cultural and Christian background, they enrich and fruitfully challenge the local church. The local church should welcome, accept and help integrate them into its life" (10).

FABC III. The Third FABC Plenary Assembly (Bangkok, Thailand, 1982) chose "The Church—A Community of Faith in Asia" as its central theme. Again, one finds enlightening words on the local Church. The final FABC III statement noted: "We have seen ... how the local church must be a community of graced communion rooted in the life of the Trinity, a community of prayer and contemplation, and of sacramental celebration and life centered around the Eucharist. It must be defined by its life of faithful discipleship in the Gospel, patterned on the Paschal Mystery of Jesus, 'a community for others.' We have realized that genuine participation and co-responsibility must be essential elements of its existence, and theological reflection and discernment integral components of its life. It is a community which strives to remain in unfeigned unity with its pastors, within the bonds of local and universal communion in the one Church" (FABC III, 15).

THESES ON THE LOCAL CHURCH. The centrality of the local Church in the theological-missiological thought in the Asian area is highlighted by the FABC commitment to study the question in depth. The FABC has promoted indigenous Asian theological reflection since its early years; the formal establishment of the Theological Advisory Commission (TAC) of the FABC came in the 1980s. A five-year period of extensive study and consultation culminated in a comprehensive document entitled "Theses on the Local Church: A Theological Reflection in the Asian Context" (TLC). This is one of the longest documents ever produced by the TAC (well over 50 closely printed pages); it was released in January 1991. In the opinion of this author, worldwide it is probably the best and most comprehensive document to date on *local Church*.

The FABC-TAC document on the local Church contains several sections. After a lengthy contextualized introduction and clarification of terms, the fifteen theses are presented in two thematic sections: "Biblical Foundations" (Theses 1-4) and "The Birth, Life and Mission of the Local Church" (Theses 5-15). Next, a concluding section follows; finally, a wide variety of practical "Pastoral Corollaries and Recommendations" are presented. Some salient quotes serve to capture the spirit of this insightful piece of Asian theological reflection on the local Church.

"Already, as we have noted, the First Plenary Assembly of the FABC spoke of building up of the local Church as the present focus of the Church's mission in Asia. That discernment remains valid today [1991]... More and more the local Churches in Asia must see themselves as responsible agents for the self-realization of the Church" (TLC: C, 3-4).

"We see the emergence of the world of the Third Millennium already upon us.... Whether the Gospel shall be present in this new age with its unpredictable turnings and its manifold diversity will depend greatly on whether local Churches fulfill their vocation in the historic moment which is now upon them. We grasp something of the significance of local Church and inculturation in this context; those who cannot understand this fail to resonate with the signs of our time, and the heartbeat of our peoples" (TLC: C, 5).

"We must surely be grateful that we experience today the 'rush of the Spirit' in our Churches. For it is a privileged moment for local theological reflection and discernment, for the gathering and spending of energies, for the upbuilding of authentic local Churches in our part of the world.... We can only pray that we may listen and be obedient to the Spirit, that we may be guided by his creative power and be filled by the commitment and courage which are his gifts" (TLC: C, 6-7).

FABC V. Most major documents of the FABC refer explicitly to the role of the local Church in mission and evangelization. The Fifth Plenary FABC Assembly held in Bandung, Indonesia (July 1990), with the theme "Journeying Together toward the Third Millennium," added new clarity and focus by asserting that it is the local Church which is "the acting subject of mission."

"The renewal of our sense of mission will mean ... that the acting subject of mission is the *local church* living and acting in communion with the universal Church. It is the local churches and communities which can discern and work out (in dialogue with each other and with other persons of goodwill) the way the Gospel is best proclaimed, the Church set up, the values of God's Kingdom realized in their own place and time. In fact, it is by responding to and serving the needs of the peoples of Asia that the different Christian communities become truly local churches" (FABC V, 3.3.1).

"This local church, which is the acting subject of mission, is the people of God in a given milieu, the whole Christian community—laity, Religious and clergy. It is the whole diocese, the parish, the Basic Ecclesial Community and other groups. Their time has come for Asia" (FABC V, 3.3.2).

FABC VI. The Sixth FABC Plenary Assembly held in Manila, Philippines in 1995 in conjunction with the visit of Pope John Paul II for the World Youth Day summarized key themes of the 25-year history of FABC. The final statement entitled "Christian Discipleship in Asia Today: Service to Life" noted that: "The overall thrust of activities in recent years has been to motivate the Churches of Asia towards 'a new way of being Church,' a Church that is committed to becoming 'a community of communities' and a credible sign of salvation and liberation" (FABC VI, 3). "It is the Spirit of Jesus that creates the [Church as a] disciple-community" (FABC VI, 14).

Many are the challenges of being an authentic local Church in Asia. Asian Catholics admit: "We may hesitate because we are a minority group. Indeed we are a little flock in Asia. But it is from this position of weakness that God's gift of divine life in Jesus Crucified, the power and wisdom of God, is most significant" (FABC VI, 14.3). Most local Churches in Asia continually discover and live their identities as minorities within their national societies.

ASIAN SYNOD ECHOES FABC THEMES. A short excursus provides interesting insights into key FABC themes about local Church that resounded in the Special Assembly for Asia of the Synod of Bishops ("Asian Synod") held in Rome from April 19-May 14, 1998. As Cardinal Stephen Kim Sou-hwan of Korea greeted the Holy Father and the Synod participants in his opening address on April 20, he described the realities of Asia which "is made up not of various nations but, one may say, many worlds."

Kim noted the endeavors and accomplishments of the FABC "for the past 27 years"; in building up a truly local Church in Asia "continual and quite serious efforts have been made to listen to, learn from, and reflect and act upon today's lived Asian realities in faith and prayer. And, we have felt called to an ever renewed self-understanding of the Church and her mission, not so much from abstract thought, but in the face of given pastoral situations and their exigencies" (OR-EE: April 29, 1998: 5).

Bishop Josef Suwatan, MSC of Indonesia asserted that the "peoples of Asia need the witness of 'being Church'." He pointed out how "the Fifth Plenary Assembly of FABC in 1990 in Bandung speaks about 'a new way of being Church' in Asia, as a 'communion of communities'."

He reiterated: "Note well, it speaks about 'being' Church!" (OR-EE: April 29, 1998: 15). Again, Archbishop Petrus Turang of Indonesia echoed the same theme and focused on the growth of the local Churches: "The Churches of Asia need to take advantage of the vision of a new way of being Church" (OR-EE: May 20, 1998: 8). This new approach will also achieve, according to Bishop John Cummins, "the desired communion among local Churches"; this means accepting "the Federation of Asian Bishops' Conferences as a vehicle to do this" (OR-EE: May 20, 1998: 13).

The missionary dimension of the local Churches of Asia emerged strongly in the Synod. Father Edward Malone, FABC Assistant Secretary General, emphasized several crucial points: "Asian Christians and local Churches have a deep sense of gratitude for the gift of faith…. With the renewal of ecclesiology a wide variety of mission initiatives must necessarily emerge from within each local Church…." Concretely, specific actions must help promote "the emergence of missionary local Churches"; thus, "pastoral care is not to derail the local Church mission effort" and "the actual foundation of Asian-born missionary societies is to be fostered in each local Church" (OR-EE: May 13, 1998: 14).

Several Synod interventions focused on the challenges of this FABC-inspired "new way of being Church." Bishop Pakiam of Malaysia captured the essence of this commitment to "be witnesses of the Gospel as a community of the local Church in a multiracial, multicultural, multilinguistic country"; note that this description reflects the reality of most Asian countries. Bishop Pakiam recommended following FABC directions so that local Churches become "a communion of communities, a participatory Church, a dialoguing and prophetic Church" (OR-EE: June 17, 1998: 8).

In the final session of the Synod on May 13, Cardinal Darmaatmadja of Indonesia again referred to the task of "being Church in Asia." For him all local Churches must struggle to be "a Church with an Asian 'face' [and an] Asian appearance"; they must avoid appearing "foreign to Asia's traditions and cultures" (OR-EE: June 17, 1998: 10-11). In a word, they must emerge as truly *local Churches*!

FABC THEMES IN *ECCLESIA IN ASIA.* The Apostolic Exhortation *Ecclesia in Asia* promulgated by Pope John Paul II in New Delhi, India on November 6, 1999 echoed the ecclesiology of the Asian Synod Fathers of the FABC region. Although the document develops the "ecclesiology of communion" extensively, significant insights on the local Churches of Asia are found within the papal exhortation.

Ecclesia in Asia notes that "the Synod Fathers were well aware of the pressing need of the local Churches in Asia to present the mystery of Christ according to their cultural patterns and ways of thinking" (20h). It is necessary that "each local Church should become what the Synod Fathers called a 'participatory Church,' a Church, that is, in which all live their proper vocation and perform their proper role" (25b). The pope's exhortation praises the Federation of Asian Bishops' Conferences by name, because it has "helped to foster union among the local Churches" and has "provided venues for cooperation in resolving pastoral problems" (26b).

In *Ecclesia in Asia* Pope John Paul II identifies important responsibilities of the local Churches in Asia: "where possible the local Churches in Asia should promote human rights activities on behalf of women" (34g); "local Churches, for their part, need to foster awareness of the ideal of the religious and consecrated life, and promote such vocations" (44c); mission is the task of each local Church, and the pope recommends "the establishment within each local Church of Asia, where such do not exist, of missionary societies of apostolic life, characterized by their special commitment to the mission *ad gentes, ad exteros* and *ad vitam*" (44d).

John Paul II continues: "the local Churches in Asia, in communion with the Successor of Peter, need to foster greater communion of mind and heart through close cooperation among themselves" (24d); while unity in the Church is essential, it also respects "the legitimate diversity of the local Churches and the variety of cultures and peoples with which they are in contact" (25a).

FABC VII. The Seventh FABC Plenary Assembly, the first major Church gathering of the Jubilee Year 2000, was held in Samphran, Thailand from January 3-12, 2000. The assembly of 193 participants (cardinals, bishops, clergy, religious, and laity) explored the theme: "A Renewed Church in Asia: A Mission of Love and Service." Once again, the integrating theology of local Church came to the fore in the final statement.

The participants asserted: "from the depths of Asia's hopes and anxieties, we hear the call of the Spirit to the local churches in Asia. It is a call to renewal, to a renewed mission of love and service. It is a call to the local churches to be faithful to Asian cultural, spiritual and social values and thus to be truly inculturated local churches" (FABC VII: Introduction).

The assembly reflected: "The thirty-year history of the FABC has been a concerted series of movements toward a renewed Church." Of the eight movements noted, one pivotal initiative has been the "movement toward a 'truly local Church,' toward a Church 'incarnate in a people, a Church indigenous and inculturated'." The assembly statement boldly affirmed: "This is the vision of a renewed Church that the FABC has developed over the past thirty years. It is still valid today" (FABC VII: I-A).

THEMATIC RECAPITULATION. This presentation has briefly sketched the development of reflection on the local Church in Asia over the past three decades. The eminent Asian theologian, Catalino G. Arévalo, SJ, has reflected on the growth of Asian local Churches in the *Jahrbuch für Kontextuelle Theologien* 1995 [1995 *Yearbook of Contextual Theologies*]. His insights in this document are worthy of extensive citation.

He notes that since the renewal of Vatican II "the Church in the FABC region was seeking increasingly to '*become* Church'.... It was an exciting time to awaken minds and hearts of Asian Christians to the real endeavor of the 'self-realization of the Church'" (31). Arévalo asserts: "For me, behind the desire for constructing local theologies [ecclesiologies] lies the 'dream of catholicity.' The catholicity of the Church has been a passion, in a way, in my mind and heart since my first contacts with ecclesiology.... It is a consequence of Incarnation and Paschal Mystery, it is the meaning of Pentecost, that (rightly understood) the realization of *catholicity* is the meaning of the Church's mission" (32).

Arévalo continues: "That means that every people, every place in Asia, has a vocation to the realization of the catholicity of the Church. Christ is 'not yet complete' until all of humanity, each part of it, has made its contribution to the 'Christ of all peoples.' Every people has its gifts and riches, and the Father has a place for all these gifts, in the Kingdom, in the Body of His Son. Equality and participation is a calling for each people in the human family. Until each people has made the contribution to the Church's unity-in-diversity which it has a right and duty to make, the work of mission of the Church has not been fulfilled" (32-33).

"My growing conviction has been that each place and region in Asia has to make its specific contribution to the mosaic which constitutes the catholicity of the Church, which in my mind is one of the most important principles of our faith. Every people has a right to find its place within the church. Every local church can only contribute to this *dream of catholicity* when it is given a status of equality and participation, because every people in the eyes of the Father is equal to all the others and has a right to be loved for themselves and for the gifts and particular contribution it can make" (33).

"Catholicity implies that we all have need of one another. That is the ultimate meaning of local church for me. A local church is never a means in itself, but in equality and participation every local church helps to bring forth the catholic communion as the ultimate aim of being church" (34).

"The Church catholic is a communion of local churches. Every local Church is a Church in a given time and place, but it is also in communion, both diachronically and synchronically, with the Church in all times and in all the world. Unless every local church shares in the *koinonia* that is the Church universal, in true equality, in authentic participation, in the interchange of gifts and blessings, the dream of catholicity has not yet been realized. It is part of our deepest duty, as Catholics especially, to help bring this to pass" (34).

An interviewer framed this question for Arévalo: "You concentrate on the *local church in Asia* as the operative agent of mission; ... do you see Asian local churches living up to the ideal that every local church is called to be a missionary, called to be a 'sending Church'?" (35).

Arévalo responded: "On the local church, this I believe must be said again and again: the concrete, operative meaning of inculturation is the process of letting the local Church be the local Church, assuming responsibility, within the *koinonia* of all the churches in the *catholica*, to 'realize itself' in its own life and mission.... Until the local Churches see their own self-realization as their duty and task, and strive to bring this about, they have not yet 'become Church' in the truest, fullest sense. Yet here in Asia, we are still a long way from that!" (35).

"The operative center of the Church's mission today is the local Church: it must discern for its own time and place what the concrete tasks of its own mission are.... We will make every effort at a renewed evangelization, but one that is truly inculturated and integral (in all dimensions of our common life). Most of our local communities are far from accomplishing these objectives" (35).

Arévalo continues in an optimistic vein: "The past twenty years of the common journey of the Asian Bishops in FABC have been years of growth for our local churches, hopefully 'in wisdom, age and grace.' In the years ahead the tasks discerned for mission remain in front of us as challenges which we have only begun to meet. *Their doing remains*" (FABC *Papers* 57*b*: 20).

CONCLUSION. The experience of the pilgrim local Churches in Asia since Vatican II has been an exciting and inspiring faith-journey. It has been an experience in ecclesiogenesis, the birthing and development of local Churches. It has verified the ancient adage that the Church is always *in via*, on the road, in process—as she awaits her Lord and Savior, Jesus Christ. The road has not been a well-trodden path; Asian Churches are making the pilgrim way in the very process of walking it—under the guidance of the befriending Spirit. Asian Christians are enthusiastic pilgrim-disciples; a renewed local Church for a new world is being born in Asia.

Local Churches, full of vitality through faith and the power of the Holy Spirit, will engage in reading the "signs of the times" (GS 4) and responding to concrete social, political, economic, religious, and cultural realities. They will foster their own inner life (inculturated faith) and be better equipped to dialogue with other Christians (ecumenism) and the followers of other faith traditions (interreligious dialogue). In short, they will experience self-actualization and "see themselves as responsible agents for the self-realization of the Church" (TLC: C-4). They will experientially know that they are "the acting subject of mission" (FABC V, 3.3.1). They will rejoice in their "new way of being Church" (FABC VI, 3).

Each local Church in Asia has received abundant and diverse gifts from the Holy Spirit. Each Church is to give freely because it has received freely (cf. Mt. 10:8). In this manner each local Church contributes to the realization of the catholicity of the Church. To cite Arévalo, "Unless every local church shares in the *koinonia* that is the Church universal, in true equality, in authentic participation, in the interchange of gifts and blessings, the dream of catholicity has not yet been realized. It is part of our deepest duty, as Catholics especially, to help bring this to pass" (*Jahrbuch*: 34). Thus, the entire Church becomes, as noted by Vatican II, the *corpus ecclesiarum* (LG 23), the body of the Churches, the corporate body of local Churches.

The Church catholic is a communion of local Churches; the Church catholic is built upon the "principle of communion" as John Paul II noted in his message to the Catholics of China from Manila in January of 1995 (OR-EE: January 18, 1995: 1). Or again, in the Catholic experience, the more that each local Church becomes truly inculturated, indigenized and localized, the more this same Church through the power of the Holy Spirit becomes universal. And, the dream of vibrant local

Churches within an authentic catholicity continues to grow and take on flesh. Christians frequently meditate on the wondrous mystery that in the power of the Spirit the Church is for believers *donum Dei atque officium nostri,* at one and the same time, both God's gift and our task!

* * *

ABBREVIATIONS

ACMC   -   Asian Colloquium on Ministries in the Church (Hong Kong, 1977) in: FAPA I: 67-92

EA   -   *Ecclesia in Asia* (The Church in Asia: November 6, 1999)

FABC   -   Federation of Asian Bishops' Conferences

FABC I   -   Evangelization in Modern Day Asia (Taipei, Taiwan, 1974) in: FAPA I: 11-25

FABC II   -   Prayer—The Life of the Church in Asia (Calcutta, India, 1978) in: FAPA I: 27-48

FABC III   -   The Church—A Community of Faith in Asia (Bangkok, Thailand, 1982) in: FAPA I: 49-65

FABC IV   -   The Vocation and Mission of the Laity in the Church and in the World of Asia (Tokyo, Japan, 1986) in: FAPA I: 177-198

FABC V   -   Journeying Together Toward the Third Millennium (Bandung, Indonesia, 1990) in: FAPA I: 273-289

FABC VI   -   Christian Discipleship in Asia Today: Service to Life (Manila, Philippines, 1995) in: FAPA II: 1-12

FABC VII - A Renewed Church in Asia: A Mission of Love and Service (Samphran, Thailand, 2000) in: FAPA III: 1-16

FAPA - *For All the Peoples of Asia*: I [1970-1991]. Edited by: Rosales, Gaudencio and Arévalo, Catalino. Maryknoll, New York: Orbis Books and Quezon City, Philippines: Claretian Publications, 1992; *For All the Peoples of Asia*: II [1992-1996]. Edited by: Eilers, Franz-Josef. Quezon City, Philippines: Claretian Publications, 1997; *For All the Peoples of Asia*: III [1997-2001]. Edited by: Eilers, Franz-Josef. Quezon City, Philippines: Claretian Publications, 2002

GS - *Gaudium et Spes* (The Church in the Modern World: December 7, 1965)

IMC - International Mission Congress (Manila, Philippines, 1979) in: FAPA I: 125-163

LG - *Lumen Gentium* (The Church: November 21, 1964)

OR-EE - *L'Osservatore Romano* (English Edition)

TAC - Theological Advisory Commission of the FABC

TLC - Theses on the Local Church (FABC *Papers* 60: 1-58)

* * *

SELECTED BIBLIOGRAPHY

THE FABC AND LOCAL CHURCH

Agustinus, B. A *Study on the Evangelizing Mission of the Church in Contemporary Asia in the Light of the Documents of the Federation of Asian Bishops' Conferences, 1970-1995.* Doctoral Thesis in Theology, Rome: Pontifical Urban University, 1997.

Amaladoss, M. "Local Churches in Asia: Problems and Prospects." *Verbum* SVD 27 (1986): 323-343.

Arévalo, C. **[A]** "The Church as a Community of Faith." FABC *Papers* 29. Hong Kong: FABC Secretariat, 1982. **[B]** "The Church in Asia and Mission in the 1990s." FABC *Papers* 57b. Hong Kong: FABC Secretariat, 1990. **[C]** "Mission in the 1990s." *International Bulletin of Missionary Research.* 14/2 (April, 1990): 50-53. **[D]** "Self-Portrait: A Life in the Service of the Church in the Philippines and of Asia." In *Jahrbuch für Kontextuelle Theologien* 1995, ed. G. Evers, 7-52. Aachen, Germany: Missionswissenschaftliches Institut Missio e.V., 1995.

Colombo, D. *Documenti della Chiesa in Asia: Federazione delle Conferenze Episcopali Asiatiche* — 1970-1995. Bologna: Editrice Missionaria Italiana, 1997.

Darmaatmadja, J. "A Church with a Truly Asian Face." *Origins* 28/2 (May 28, 1998): 24-28.

Dulles, A. and P. Granfield. "The Particular or Local Church" 132-135 and "Asian Ecclesiology" 173-174. In *The Theology of the Church: A Bibliography.* New York: Paulist Press, 1999.

Eilers, F. ed. **[A]** *For All the Peoples of Asia: Federation of Asian Bishops' Conferences Documents from 1992 to 1996.*

Quezon City, Philippines: Claretian Publications, 1997. **[B]** *For All the Peoples of Asia: Federation of Asian Bishops' Conferences Documents from 1997 to 2001.* Quezon City, Philippines: Claretian Publications, 2002.

Emmanuel, S. **[A]** "Local Churches and the World Church." *East Asian Pastoral Review* 27/1 (1990): 59-75. **[B]** "Asian Churches for a New Evangelization: Chances and Challenges." *East Asian Pastoral Review* 36/3 (1999): 252-275.

Evers, G., ed. *Bibliography on Local Church in Asia* [*Theology in Context Supplements* 3]. Aachen, Germany: Institute of Missiology, 1989.

FABC:TAC (Federation of Asian Bishops' Conferences: Theological Advisory Commission). "Theses on the Local Church: A Theological Reflection in the Asian Context." In *Being Church in Asia,* ed. J. Gnanapiragasam and F. Wilfred, 33-89. Quezon City, Philippines: Claretian Publications, 1994 [See: FABC *Papers* 60: 1-58].

Fitzpatrick, M. *Bishop Francisco F. Claver, SJ on the Local Church* (1972-1990). Manila: De La Salle University Press, Inc., 1995 [Extensive Bibliography].

Fox, T. *Pentecost in Asia: A New Way of Being Church.* Maryknoll, New York: Orbis Books, 2002.

Handoko, P. *Lay Ministries in the Mission and Ministry of the Church in Asia: A Critical Study of the Documents of the FABC, 1970-1991.* Doctoral Thesis in Theology, Rome: Pontifical Gregorian University, 1993.

Hardawiryana, R. "The Missionary Dimensions of the Local Church: Asia and Indonesia." In *Mission in Dialogue,* ed. M. Motte and J. Lang, 34-72. Maryknoll, New York: Orbis Books, 1982.

Hennesey, J. "The Ecclesiology of the Local Church: A Historian's Look." *Thought* 66/263 (December, 1991): 368-375.

Heyndrickx, J. "The Emergence of a Local Catholic Church in China?" *Tripod* 37 (1987): 51-75.

Kavunkal, J. "Local Church in the FABC Statements." *Jeevadhara* 27/160 (1997): 260-271.

Keeler, W. "Bishops' Conferences: Servants of Communion between the Local and Universal Church." *Origins* 31/18 (October 11, 2001): 304-306.

Komonchak, J. **[A]** "The Church Universal as the Communion of Local Churches." In *Where Does the Church Stand?* ed. G. Alberigo and G. Gutierrez, 30-35. New York: The Seabury Press, 1981. **[B]** "Towards a Theology of the Local Church." FABC *Papers* 42. Hong Kong: FABC Secretariat, 1986. **[C]** "The Local Realization of the Church." In *The Reception of Vatican II.* ed. G. Alberigo et al., 77-90 Washington, D.C.: The Catholic University of America Press, 1987. **[D]** "The Church: God's Gift and Our Task." *Origins* 16/42 (April 2, 1987): 735-741. **[E]** "The Local Church." *Chicago Studies* 28/3 (November, 1989): 320-335. **[F]** "Many Models, One Church." *Church* 9/1 (Spring, 1993): 12-15.

Kroeger, J. **[A]** *Living Mission: Challenges in Evangelization Today.* Maryknoll, New York: Orbis Books and Quezon City, Philippines: Claretian Publications, 1994. **[B]** "Missionary Work in Asia." *Catholic International* 7/8-9 (August-September, 1996): 421-423. **[C]** *Asia-Church in Mission.* Quezon City, Philippines: Claretian Publications, 1999. **[D]** "Rejoice, O Asia-Church!" *East Asian Pastoral Review* 37/3 (2000): 278-285. **[E]** "A Continuing Pentecost: Appreciating 'Ecclesia in Asia'." *Review for Religious* 60/1 (January-February, 2001): 20-29. **[F]** J. Kroeger and P. Phan, ed. *The Future of the Asian Churches: The Asian Synod and Ecclesia in Asia.* Quezon City, Philippines: Claretian Publications, 2002.

LaRousse, W. *Urgency for Mission in the Local Church.* Licentiate Thesis in Missiology, Rome: Pontifical Gregorian University, 1997 [Extensive Bibliography].

Legrand, H. *The Local Church and Catholicity* [The *Jurist* 52/1 (1992): 1-586]. Washington, D.C.: The Catholic University of America, 1992.

Malone, E. "Contribution of the Federation of Asian Bishops' Conferences (FABC) to the Evangelizing Mission of the Church in Asia." In *Telling God's Story*, ed. J. Kroeger, 127-132. Quezon City, Philippines: Claretian Publications, 2001.

Marriage, S. "The Place of the Local Church in the Liberation/Inculturation Debate: The Infanta Prelature Experience." *East Asian Pastoral Review* 37/1 (2000): 83-102.

Nocent, A. "The Local Church as Realization of the Church of Christ and Subject of the Eucharist." In *The Reception of Vatican II*, ed. G. Alberigo et al., 215-229. Washington, D.C.: The Catholic University of America Press, 1987.

Phan, P. *Christianity with an Asian Face.* Maryknoll, New York: Orbis Books, 2003.

Pieris, A. "Asia's Non-Semitic Religions and the Mission of Local Churches." In *An Asian Theology of Liberation*, 35-50. Maryknoll, New York: Orbis Books, 1988.

Quatra, M. *At the Side of the Multitudes: The Kingdom of God and the Mission of the Church in the FABC Documents (1970-1995).* Quezon City, Philippines: Claretian Publications, 2000.

Quevedo, O. **[A]** "The Basic Ecclesial Community as a Church Model for Asia." In *A Church on the Threshold*, ed. M. Seigel, 193-204. Rome: SEDOS, 1998. **[B]** "Steps Toward Renewing the Church in Asia." *Origins* 29/34 (February 10, 2000): 545, 547-548.

Rosales, G. and C. Arévalo, ed. *For All the Peoples of Asia: Federation of Asian Bishops' Conferences Documents from 1970 to 1991.* Maryknoll, New York: Orbis Books and Quezon City, Philippines: Claretian Publications, 1992 and 1997.

Rossignol, R. "Vatican II and Missionary Responsibility of the Particular Churches." *Indian Theological Studies* 17/1 (March, 1980): 34-46.

Salm, L. *The Local Church: Proceedings of the Thirty-Sixth Annual Convention.* Bronx, New York: The Catholic Theological Society of America, 1982.

Tagle, L. "The Renewal that Awaits the Church in Asia." In *It Is the Lord!* 69-92. Manila: Loyola School of Theology, 2003.

Tan Yun-ka, J. **[A]** "Constructing an Asian Theology of Liturgical Inculturation from the Documents of the Federation of Asian Bishops' Conferences [FABC]." *East Asian Pastoral Review* 36/4 (1999): 383-401. **[B]** "*Missio ad Gentes*" in Asia: A Comparative Study of the Missiology of John Paul II and the Federation of Asian Bishops' Conferences. Doctoral Thesis in Theology, Washington, D.C.: The Catholic University of America, 2002.

Tillard, J. *Church of Churches: The Ecclesiology of Communion* (*Église d' Églises:* 1987) Collegeville, Minnesota: The Liturgical Press, 1992.

Wilfred, F. et al. "What the Spirit Says to the Churches (Rev 2:7): A Vademecum on the Pastoral and Theological Orientations of the Federation of Asian Bishops' Conferences (FABC)." *Vidyajyoti* 62/2 (February, 1998): 124-133.

3

A CHURCH LIVING TO EVANGELIZE

Recent Popes and Integral Evangelization

Evangelization, for many Catholics, is a generally unfamiliar and relatively new term; only recently has it been gaining wider currency. The Second Vatican Council as well as recent popes have placed evangelization at the center of the Church's identity and mission. The goal of this presentation is to focus specifically on the unique contributions of Paul VI and John Paul II to the understanding of evangelization in all of its rich, complex, multi-faceted, and interrelated dimensions. In a word, this piece explores evangelization viewed holistically and integrally.

The word "evangelization" does not occur in the New Testament; however, *euaggelion* meaning "gospel" or "good news" occurs 72 times, 54 of which are in the Pauline corpus. It has a wide range of meanings: the whole Christian message (Mk 1:1); the good news of Jesus (II Cor 4:4); it is for all (Mk 13:10; 16:15); it is a revelation of God (Gal 1:11-12) which is to be believed (Mk 1:15) and proclaimed (I Cor 9:14, 16, 18). One must risk all for the gospel (Mk 8:35; Rom 1:16), serve it (Rom 1:1; 15:16), defend it (Phil 1:7, 16). *Euaggelion* is the good news of truth (Gal 2:5, 14), of hope (Col 1:23), of peace (Eph 6:15), of immortality (II Tim 1:10), of the risen Christ (I Cor 15:1ff; II Tim 2:8), and of salvation (Eph 1:13).

Vatican II speaks of evangelization in a variety of contexts: it is especially the bishops' task to promote evangelization by the faithful (CD 6); it is associated with the mission of the laity (AA 2, 6, 20, 26; LG 35); priests are to learn the methods of evangelization (PO 19); the Eucharist is the source and summit of all evangelization (PO 5). The Decree on Missions (AG) is replete with references: "the specific purpose of missionary activity is evangelization and the planting of the Church" (6); "the Church has the obligation and the sacred right to evangelize" (7); catechists have an important task to evangelize (17), as do the laity (21); the call to evangelize arises from a charism of the Spirit (23); various roles are fulfilled by missionary institutes (27), Propaganda Fidei (29), the people of God (35, 36), bishops and priests (38), religious institutes (40), and young Churches (LG 17).

Following upon a solid foundation in Sacred Scripture and in the documents of Vatican II, the pivotal contribution of Paul VI and John Paul II has been to locate evangelization on "center-stage" in describing the Church's contemporary mission. An obvious question arises: How does one capture the rich thought of these two popes? This author takes the path of an extensive presentation of the seminal document of each pope on the subject of evangelization. Thus, this presentation unfolds in three lengthy interrelated sections: **I.** Paul VI and *Evangelii Nuntiandi*; **II.** John Paul II and *Redemptoris Missio*; and, **III.** Synthetic Overview of Integral Evangelization.

I. Paul VI and **Evangelii Nuntiandi**

Pope Paul VI (1963-1978) will always be remembered as a modern missionary pope; he made missionary journeys to all continents; he authored *Evangelii Nuntiandi* (EN), which became the *magna carta* for Catholic evangelization in the last quarter of the second millennium of Christianity. Without doubt, EN is one of the most important ecclesial documents of the post-Vatican II era. It presents a concise, inspiring, and programmatic challenge for the Church to enthusiastically engage in her God-given mission to preach the Gospel to the contemporary world—to living peoples, with their aspirations and anxieties, their cultures and religions, their hopes and conflicts. EN boldly addresses the topic of evangelization in the modern world.

BACKGROUND. EN, a document of 23,000 words, was issued on December 8, 1975; it emerged from several rich sources and antecedents. Very few recent papal documents have been prepared with so much prior consultation with so many different sections of the Church over so long a time period. To understand the context and content of EN, it is necessary to examine the events surrounding the 1974 International Synod on Evangelization (Paul VI explicitly refers to the Synod over 30 times in EN).

The Synod (September 27-October 26, 1974) brought together over 200 bishops from all parts of the world, along with some priests, religious, and laity in a consultative capacity. Three full years had been devoted to preparations on local, national, and continental levels. Pastoral experiences and approaches to evangelization were widely shared; the method was decidedly an inductive (not deductive) approach. The Churches in the so-called Third World devoted much effort and enthusiasm to the process. One fine example was the dedicated commitment of the Federation of Asian Bishops' Conferences (FABC); their First Plenary Assembly (April 1974: Taipei, Taiwan) produced the insightful document: *Evangelization in Modern Day Asia*.

When the 209 bishops arrived in Rome in late 1974, they were well prepared, ready and enthusiastic to engage in the Synod's work. Pope Paul VI opened the Synod with a Eucharist celebrated in the Sistine chapel; he also delivered an opening address, encouraging frank discussion and honest exchange on the burning issues surrounding evangelization. Paul VI had set the stage; he faithfully attended all the general assemblies as a silent but attentive listener.

The Synod proceeded according to its three planned stages: **(a)** *communication of pastoral experiences*; these included five continental reports and about 175 speeches of Synod Fathers; **(b)** *reflection on interrelated theological themes*; an attempt was made to integrate theological elements and pastoral experiences; it met difficulties and revealed many lacunae; **(c)** *preparation of conclusions*; working with an immense amount of material and items prepared by D. Grasso, C. Wojtyla, and D.S. Amalorpavadass, a drafting committee prepared a 41-page text.

On October 22 (just four days before the Synod's conclusion) three-quarters of the text was rejected; it had failed to capture the testimonies and insights, the searchings and propositions that characterized the first three weeks of Synod work. Thus, the final session of the Synod (October 26, 1974) was awaited with keen interest. Pope Paul VI addressed the assembly frankly and openly: "the synod of bishops has ended.... We should want to assess its achievements.... We cannot but be genuinely satisfied and optimistic about its outcome."

The pope continued: "The theme [of evangelization] is too wide and complex to be dealt with properly in so short a time or to yield all the conclusions to which its discussion might give rise. However, this Synod did again make the following contribution to the Church in our day: it enabled the voices of the local churches to be heard; it facilitated a better diagnosis of the current situation and a delineation of the principal elements of evangelization; it set in train the discussion of the practice and theory of evangelization in our time. For this reason we judge that the Synod as a whole has been fruitful. For it places at the disposal of Peter's successor, for the benefit of the entire Church, an abundance of advice, admonitions and proposals."

EVANGELII NUNTIANDI **EMERGES.** During a year-long gestation period, Pope Paul VI labored to produce from the rich experience and insights of the Synod a document that is clearly the work of discernment and synthesis. EN is at once synodal and papal and therefore deeply collegial. EN is structured in seven thematic chapters and framed with an introduction and conclusion. Chapter titles clearly indicate specific content (e.g. "What is Evangelization?" "The Methods of Evangelization"). The five-paragraph introduction contains several interpretive keys to the document.

Paul VI clearly saw his role in shaping EN to be part of his papal responsibility of "encouraging our brethren in their mission as evangelizers"; this task became for him "a daily preoccupation ... and a fundamental commitment of our Pontificate" (1). What emerged as EN has been described as Paul VI's "last and finest apostolic exhortation, a novel and effective form of the magisterium."

Secondly, EN was not written as a tightly reasoned and carefully nuanced theological treatise (although

excellent theological reflection pervades the document).
Paul VI notes that his words are designed to be a
"meditation on evangelization"; he hopes that they will
succeed "in inviting the whole People of God assembled
in the Church to make the same meditation" (5). The
pope returns to the theme of meditation throughout
EN (cf. 40, 76). It is this very personal, even conver-
sational, style of meditative reflection and exhortation
that many have found attractive; it invites a frequent
return to EN—even 25 years later. It encourages personal
reception and assimilation of the message; it exudes a
poetic quality.

Paul VI notes that three key elements converge to
highlight the importance of the promulgation of EN (2):
the conclusion of the Holy Year (a special time of
renewal); the tenth anniversary of the close of Vatican II
(renewing the Church for mission); and, the first
anniversary of the 1974 Synod. The pope again alludes
to these anniversaries in the conclusion of EN, adding
that the Church stands at "the eve of a new century, the
eve also of the third millennium of Christianity" (81).
Clearly, Paul VI wishes to focus the entire attention of
the Church on the centrality of evangelization. He wishes
to launch "a new period of evangelization" (2) so that
Christ's followers "can bring the Christian message to
modern man" (3) "with ever increasing love, zeal and joy"
(1). Fulfillment of this task is for the pope, "our heartfelt
plea" (81).

Three leitmotifs of EN have already been
mentioned: the papal commitment to evangelization, the
role of meditation, and the centrality of evangelization
in the life of the Church. A fourth theme centers on
fidelity, a double fidelity—to God's message and to
people (cf. 4, 39, 63). This fidelity is "the central axis of
evangelization" (4). In numerous places throughout EN,

Paul VI carefully defines, nuances, and balances diverse elements within the evangelization process (e.g. local and universal Church, culture and faith, liberation and evangelization, strengths and limitations of popular religiosity, etc.). It is the unique genius of Paul VI to have achieved integration and balance on so many topics. Thus, *Evangelii Nuntiandi* prolongs the reflection on evangelization begun in the 1974 Synod and makes its insights available to the entire Church. Paul VI has gifted the Church with an inspirational and pastoral handbook for modern missionary activity.

DESCRIBING EVANGELIZATION. The understanding of the term "evangelization" found in EN reflects a comprehensive and inclusive view; its use may be described as an "umbrella concept." This broad and holistic view respects the fullness and complexity of the evangelizing process, aiming to achieve *effective* evangelization.

Sections 17 and 24 provide a long list of the various elements comprising the evangelizing action of the Church. Both sections also strongly insist upon integrating and balancing all facets of evangelization. "Any partial and fragmentary definition which attempts to render the reality of evangelization in all its richness, complexity and dynamism does so only at the risk of impoverishing it and even distorting it" (17). "Evangelization, as we have said, is a complex process made up of varied elements; ... they are complementary and mutually enriching" (24).

Paul VI explicitly notes that the Synod constantly challenged the Church "to relate these elements rather than to place them in opposition one to the other, in order to reach a full understanding of the Church's evangelizing activity" (24). The pope has, in fact, set forth in EN a comprehensive presentation which in later years has become widely accepted in the Church; it is diversely termed "integral / holistic" and coupled with "evangelization / liberation / salvation."

Note the broad and inclusive manner in which Paul VI speaks: "evangelizing means bringing the Good News into all the strata of humanity" (18); "upsetting, through the power of the Gospel, mankind's criteria of judgment" (19); "what matters is to evangelize man's culture and cultures" (20) so as to overcome "the split between the Gospel and culture [which] is without doubt the drama of our time" (20). The scope of evangelization extends to the full transformation of humanity and cultures in the light of the Gospel. Additional examples from the pope's writings could be mentioned, all illustrating Paul VI's broad and holistic view of evangelization. Here, then, is a key, a helpful category, a foundational insight, for an integrated interpretation of the entire text of EN.

THEOLOGICAL FOUNDATIONS. Viewing evangelization holistically and integrally has important practical and pastoral ramifications. It allows Christians to appreciate the myriad manifestations of evangelization; individual gifts, talents, and charisms are desired and treasured (66); no individual or group is master of evangelization (15, 78); everyone acts "in communion with the Church" (60); "the work of evangelization is a basic duty of the People of God" (59).

These practical and pastoral dimensions of an integral approach to evangelization have as their basis solid theological foundations. They are anchored in "the Father's love" (26), in the entire life, mission, practice, and witness of Jesus, "the first evangelizer" (7, cf. 6-12). The Church "is born of the evangelizing activity of Jesus and the Twelve"; she "in her turn is sent by Jesus" (15). In the power of the Spirit, "the Apostles depart to all the ends of the earth in order to begin the great work of the Church's evangelization" (75). A brief look at the footnote references of the first two chapters of EN reveals how closely these theological foundations are linked with Sacred Scripture and the documents of the Second Vatican Council.

EN contains several beautiful descriptions of the Church as an evangelizing community. "Evangelization is in fact the grace and vocation proper to the Church, her deepest identity. She exists in order to evangelize"; "evangelizing all people constitutes the essential mission of the Church" (14). "The Church is an evangelizer, but she begins by being evangelized herself" (15).

Paul VI makes an important clarification in the first section of Chapter III: "The Content of Evangelization." He speaks of the distinction between the *essential* elements and the "living substance" of the Gospel message, and the *secondary* elements "whose presentation depends greatly on changing situations" (25). Within an integral view of evangelization, one must have a clear mind on the vital substance (26-28) in relation to the secondary aspects (29-39). Once again, the principle of "double fidelity" (4) enters; "evangelization would not be complete if it did not take account of the unceasing interplay of the Gospel and of man's concrete life, both personal and social" (29). In the mind of Paul VI, this continued nuancing and balanced integration are certainly part of the "drama of fidelity" (39).

DIVERSE SYNOD THEMES. It has been noted that the 1974 Synod on Evangelization ended inconclusively and that the entire documentation of the proceedings was left in the pope's hands. EN reveals how Paul VI, not wishing the material to be lost, reworked many of the Synod's major themes into a stirring and unified presentation.

He addresses several questions in the mode of a pastoral synthesis: salvation and liberation (9, 27, 30-38), non-Christian religions (53, 80), religious liberty (39, 80), secularization (55), secularism (55-56), atheism (54-56), ecumenism (54, 76, 77), basic communities (58), diversified ministries (73), popular piety (48), sacraments in evangelization (23, 28, 47, 68), mass media (45, 80), Church as sign and sacrament of salvation (23, 59), violence (37), signs of the times (75-76), the local-universal Church dynamic (60-68), culture (20, 58), and the role of the Holy Spirit (75, 82).

Many of these diverse topics had been identified by Paul VI in his final Synod speech as areas of evangelization needing to be "better defined, nuanced, completed and subjected to further study." Commentators have noted how closely certain passages in EN resemble the actual interventions made on the Synod floor. Thus, EN is a testimony that Paul VI was involved as an intent listener and learner at the Synod; then, through his papal "charism of discernment" he fashioned his insights and reflections into a personal and spiritual testament on evangelization. EN is the fruit of long and profound meditation; it nourishes the spiritual life.

SPECIAL THEMES. This summary overview of the scope of evangelization found in EN presents only the highlights of this dense and rich document. Some special themes deserve additional comment.

EN is an important document in two ways for the emerging theology of the *local Church*. It presents a basically positive and firm link between the local and the universal Church. It also shows the importance that the local community and its personal witnesses have in the whole process of inculturated evangelization. Basic ecclesial communities (58) have enormous potential to manifest the missionary character of the Church.

EN contains few direct references to *the missions*, as they were traditionally known. Where do missionary societies and organizations find their place in the contemporary world? In the fifth chapter, three specific tasks are mentioned; missionaries are to: **(a)** proclaim the Gospel for the first time to peoples and lands where it has not been heard (51); **(b)** engage and interact with the faithful adherents of other religions (53); and **(c)** assist the young Churches and promote missionary consciousness within them (56, 58).

The treatment of *world religions* in EN is not sufficiently developed. This is remarkable in a document authored by Paul VI whose first encyclical *Ecclesiam Suam* was dedicated to the theme of dialogue and who established the Secretariat for non-Christians in 1964. Several reasons for respecting and esteeming these religions are mentioned (53), but there is no theological understanding of religions in EN (Are non-Christians saved *in* and *through* their religions? Can these faith-traditions be called "ways of salvation"?). The openness expressed at the Synod which affirmed the wide action of the Holy Spirit and expressed the desire for interreligious dialogue is not pursued or promoted in EN; the term "dialogue" is not found in all of EN. In any case, one can be grateful for the encouragement given to foster an open and respectful attitude towards the great religions of the world.

The role that EN assigns to the promotion of *justice and human liberation* within the Church's evangelizing mission is a curious one. Many helpful clarifications on the concept of liberation are presented (29-39). EN notes that "Between evangelization and human advancement—development and liberation—there are in fact profound links" (31). Yet, to say that liberation "is not foreign to evangelization" (30) seems restrictive; this stands in contrast to the 1971 Synod that declared justice to be "a constitutive dimension of the preaching of the Gospel."

IMPACT ON THE CHURCH. The Synod and EN have profoundly influenced the Church; they provided the inspiration, emphasis, and methodology to place evangelization in center spotlight in the Church. National and continental Church gatherings were inspired by EN; "Evangelization at Present and in the Future of Latin America" (CELAM: Puebla, 1979) is only one of many examples.

EN influenced the methodology of subsequent synods (the synod proper followed later by a post-synodal document) as well as their topics of discussion (e.g. catechesis, family, reconciliation, etc.). EN also affirmed key Vatican II documents (*Lumen Gentium*, *Gaudium et Spes*, and *Ad Gentes*) and promoted their reception and implementation in the Church.

The Synod and EN manifested the positive contribution of "third-world" local Churches; the benefits of an inductive, collegial, and reflective method of theologizing were highlighted. The emergence of a truly "World Church" received forward impetus. Missionary journeys, begun by Paul VI, have become a common papal *modus operandi*.

The Church has renewed her commitment to being a community of disciples and evangelizers (13, 15, 21, 24, 59, 66, 80), filled with joy and enthusiasm (73, 80), eager to give authentic witness (41, 76), under the dynamic action of the Holy Spirit, the principal agent of evangelization (75) and guided by Mary, the Star of Evangelization (82).

II. John Paul II and *Redemptoris Missio*

Karol Jósef Wojtyla was elected pope on October 16, 1978 and took the name John Paul II. Under his leadership the papal ministry has become focused on evangelization and global mission, as he travels to numerous countries, strengthens local Christian communities, encounters followers of other religions, speaks on the social teachings of the Church, canonizes saints and honors blesseds, meets with youth and government leaders. Pope John Paul II asserts that the Second Vatican Council has set the direction for his papacy; he has enunciated a clear vision for the Church in the third Christian millennium.

GIFT OF A MISSION ENCYCLICAL. John Paul II's eighth encyclical *Redemptoris Missio* (RM) was issued on December 7, 1990; it celebrates the twenty-fifth anniversary of Vatican II's Mission Decree *Ad Gentes* and the fifteenth anniversary of Paul VI's *Evangelii Nuntiandi*. In RM, the pope sounds a clarion and urgent call to all Church sectors to renew their enthusiasm and commitment to evangelize the world. Composed of eight chapters plus an introduction (1-3) and conclusion (92), RM has a "doctrinal" section (4-30) and a "pastoral" section (31-91), respectively treating the "Why" and "How" of contemporary mission / evangelization.

John Paul II begins by stating his conviction about "the *urgency of missionary activity*, a subject to which I am devoting the present Encyclical" (1). The Pope asserts: "Missionary activity specifically directed *ad gentes* [to the nations] appears to be waning." This fact "must arouse concern among all who believe in Christ." Why? Because "in the Church's history, missionary drive has always been a sign of vitality, just as its lessening is a sign of a crisis of faith" (2).

The Pope urges a "fresh impulse to missionary activity," the deepening of "commitment of the particular churches," and the harnessing of "all of the Church's energies to a new evangelization" (2-3). In a word, the focus of John Paul II is direct and clear: "I wish to invite the Church to *renew her missionary commitment*" (2). All are invited to participate: "*Peoples everywhere, open the doors to Christ!*" (3).

VISION OF EVANGELIZATION. What view of evangelization emerges from a comprehensive analysis of the encyclical? Repeatedly, the document speaks of mission, evangelization and salvation in a holistic fashion: "Jesus came to bring integral salvation, one which embraces the whole person" (11); "evangelical witness ... is directed towards integral human development" (42); "action on behalf of integral development and liberation ... is most urgently needed" (58).

Integral evangelization, as repeatedly affirmed in the encyclical (20, 41-60), reflects current missiological thought as well as recent magisterial teaching. As already noted, Paul VI in EN clearly encouraged Catholics to view evangelization holistically; the second chapter of EN speaks of the complexity of the evangelizing action and its various complementary and mutually enriching elements. RM echoes this vision: "Mission is a single but complex reality, and it develops in a variety of ways" (41). Again, "mission is one and undivided, having one origin and one final purpose; but within it, there are different tasks and kinds of activity" (31). This is the vision of evangelization that the pope consistently promotes throughout RM.

FOUNDATIONAL MISSION THEOLOGY. RM clearly affirms the foundations of mission theology and the centrality and urgency of mission in the life of the Church. The years following the Second Vatican Council were a golden opportunity to explore and debate, renew and clarify the Church's mission; and, it is true that the Council "has already borne much fruit in the realm of missionary activity.... Above all, there is a new awareness that *missionary activity is a matter for all Christians*" (2). Yet, John Paul II also discerned a need to reaffirm diverse aspects of the Catholic Church's foundational theology of Christian mission and evangelization.

At least one third of the encyclical (three chapters out of eight) deals with theological questions. Chapter One includes core elements of the dogmatic theology of Revelation and Faith, Christology and Soteriology, as well as Ecclesiology and Missiology. Chapter Two focuses on biblical theology, particularly the Kingdom of God. And, to the delight of missiologists, Chapter Three is completely devoted to Pneumatology, examining the role of the Holy Spirit in the life of the Church and her evangelizing mission.

The following are key emphases in the opening chapter: **(a)** All mission is centered in God's wonderful, generous loving plan of salvation (*mysterion*), made known through Jesus and accepted in faith. Jesus is the "definitive self-revelation of God" and "the fundamental reason why the Church is missionary by her very nature" (5). **(b)** While affirming with the Scriptures (I Tim 2:4) the universality of salvation, "the Church believes that God has established Christ as the one mediator and that it has been established as the universal sacrament of salvation" (9). **(c)** The Pope unhesitatingly reaffirms these basics of Church teaching, noting that "*Mission is an issue of faith*" (11).

The biblical theme of the Kingdom (*basileia*) is the integrating leitmotif of the second chapter. Preaching the Kingdom and promoting its values are the evangelizing tasks of the Church which is "effectively and

concretely at the service of the Kingdom" (20). The
encyclical offers clarity and interpretation on other
dimensions of Kingdom theology: the Kingdom of God
and the Christ-event are complementary proclamations
(16); the Kingdom necessarily has a transcendent horizon
(17); the Kingdom "cannot be detached either from Christ
or from the Church" (18); theocentrism and
ecclesiocentrism demand a nuanced critique which is
consistent with Church teaching (17-18).

Currently, the theology of the Holy Spirit
(Pneumatology) is of particular interest to missiologists
and missionaries alike. "The Holy Spirit is indeed the
principal agent of the whole of the Church's mission of
evangelization. The Holy Spirit's action is preeminent in
mission *ad gentes*" (21). The Spirit's centrality is
emphasized because the Holy Spirit's "presence and
activity affect not only individuals but also society and
history, peoples, cultures and religions" (28). Ask any
missionary and you will receive an eloquent personal
testimony of the presence and power of the Spirit active
in peoples, cultures, and religions—renewing the face of
the earth! The acts of today's apostles continuously write
the gospel of the Holy Spirit!

TRANSMITTING THE URGENCY OF MISSION.
The English subtitle given to RM is: "On the Permanent
Validity of the Church's Missionary Mandate." Thus,
mission is always and everywhere essential; it is "not
considered a marginal task for the Church but is
situated at the center of her life, as a fundamental
commitment of the whole People of God" (32). Mission
is "the greatest and holiest duty of the Church" (63). The
Pope's affirmations resonate throughout the work: "I
have chosen to travel to the ends of the earth in order
to show this missionary concern" (1); "mission *ad gentes*
is still in its infancy" (40); "I see the dawning of a new
missionary age" (92).

No one seeks to minimize the Pope's assertions about the centrality and urgency of missionary evangelization; however, it is a valid question to ask about strategies for implementation. Words of exhortation must give way to programs of concrete actualization. In the considered judgment of this author, the encyclical is strong on the *why* of mission, but is only moderately successful on the *how*. Mission animation—the *how* of mission—requires continued discussion. While it is best accomplished locally, within the local Church, one can highlight some creative suggestions found within RM.

The Christian family is a key and irreplaceable force in evangelization (42); this insight is consistent with the teaching of Vatican II which termed the family the "domestic church" (LG 11). Promoting Christian family life should redound to mission awareness and animation. Material and financial donations are gratefully received, yet families are challenged to offer "a special contribution to the missionary cause of the Church by fostering missionary vocations among their sons and daughters" (80).

John Paul II challenges Christians: Do you wish to promote mission? True disciples are urged to "carry out a sincere review of their lives regarding their solidarity with the poor" (60). As followers of Jesus, "we should reassess our own way of living" (81); "Fight hunger by changing your lifestyle" (59); "We cannot preach conversion unless we ourselves are converted anew every day" (47).

The role of missionary institutes and societies is crucial in worldwide evangelization; missionaries themselves should continue their "radical and total self-giving," initiate "new and bold endeavors," and "not allow themselves to be daunted by doubts, misunderstanding, rejection or persecution" (66).

Diocesan seminarians and priests "must have the mind
and heart of missionaries" (67). The Church must seek
to expand the spheres "in which lay people are present
and active as missionaries" (72). Missionary dynamism
should become contagious!

Youth involvement is essential to mission and
evangelization. They should be offered opportunities to
visit overseas missions, to meet and offer hospitality to
non-Christians and migrants within their own country
(82). The idealism of youth is a potential resource—their
rejection of violence and war, their desire for freedom
and justice, their rejection of racism and closed
nationalism, their affirmation of the dignity and role of
women (86). The vision of Charles de Foucauld (as a
"universal brother") can fire the imagination of youth (89),
can be a path toward missionary commitment.

ADDITIONAL MAJOR EMPHASES. In composing
a popular overview of a papal encyclical one faces the
challenge of providing a balanced presentation. This
writer sees several other major emphases on
evangelization within the work; he devotes a paragraph
to each theme.

Around the world *local churches* are the central actors
in mission today; all evangelization necessarily is
harmoniously accomplished in, with, and through the
local Church which is responsible for the totality of
mission. This is a sea change in the dynamics of mission;
both local Churches and missionaries alike must explore
the ramifications of this new reality. Many leads are
found in the encyclical (26, 30, 39, 48-52, 62-64, 71, 83-
85, 92).

Authentic evangelization is a *freely-offered gift*, not an
external imposition which violates human dignity and
freedom. Or again, witnessing and proclaiming Christ
are not at odds with people's dignity as persons or their

freedom of conscience (7-8). Genuine mission does not restrict freedom, but rather seeks to advance it; RM is clear: *"The Church proposes; she imposes nothing"* (39).

The Church needs *missionary vocations*. Individuals who receive the permanent, life-long vocation to foreign, transcultural mission are a treasured resource of the Church. Their vocation is necessary for the Church (32); it is a unique calling (27, 65); it is the model of the Church's missionary commitment (66); it is to be assiduously cultivated (79, 84), particularly by mission institutes themselves (65-66).

The encyclical looks positively upon *interreligious dialogue*, devoting several sections to presenting it comprehensively (55-57). Interfaith dialogue "is part of the Church's evangelizing mission, ... is not in opposition to the mission *ad gentes*, ... |and| *does not dispense from evangelization."* This same section (55) speaks of God's call to all peoples and his presence to them "of which their religions are the main and essential expression." The Church's reverence for the followers of other faiths and religions is clearly affirmed by the encyclical.

In RM *women* receive the Pope's praise and gratitude for their outstanding contribution to evangelization: "I extend a special word of appreciation to the missionary Religious sisters" (70); "How can we forget the important role played by women"? (71). "It is necessary to recognize—and it is a title of honor—that some Churches owe their origins to the activity of lay men and women missionaries" (71).

The process of *inculturation* and its relationship to mission receives extensive treatment (25, 52-54, 76). Authentic evangelization involves the Church in the inculturation process, an "intimate transformation of authentic cultural values through their integration in Christianity and the insertion of Christianity in the various human cultures." This task is never finished and today it encounters new challenges—especially in large cities, "where new customs and styles of living arise together with new forms of culture and communication" (37). Mission and inculturation demand fresh initiatives and creativity in the techtronic age of the megalopolis!

The entire final chapter of *Redemptoris Missio* treats *missionary spirituality* (87-91). Four elements characterize Jesus' disciples-become-missionary: the missionary is to be led by the Spirit, to live the mystery of Christ who himself was sent, to love the Church and humanity as Jesus did, and to desire the holiness of saints. In a word, mission spirituality is "a journey towards holiness" (90) and the success of renewing the urgency of the Church's missionary impulse "demands holy missionaries" (90).

PRECIOUS DETAILS—NOT TO BE LOST. In a work as long as RM one expects to find several details that demand further reflection. This synthesis presentation takes note of five additional themes and their importance for evangelization.

The *personalist philosophy* and orientation of John Paul II is manifested throughout the work. The person is always central in evangelization and all mission apostolates: in work for justice (42), in fostering interreligious dialogue (55-57), in promoting development; the human person "is the principal agent of development, not money or technology" (58). In uniquely personalist terms, the missionary is described as "a person of the Beatitudes" (91) and it is personal love that is always "*the driving force of mission*" (60).

The encyclical profusely expresses the *Church's gratitude* to its missionaries (2, 57, 60, 70). The Church's theologians provide an important service to the cause of evangelization (36) and should promote the study of world religions and science of missiology (83). The

Church needs a renewed commitment to ecumenism within mission (50).

In looking at today's world from the viewpoint of evangelization, the document distinguishes *three situations*: "non-Christian" peoples, Christians requiring pastoral care, and the so-called "post-Christians"; all require special approaches (32-34). Geographically, the Pope emphasizes the missionary demands within Asia (37, 55, 91).

Significant and surprising is the fact that *one unique quote* appears verbatim no less than three times in the text (6, 10, 28): "we are obliged to hold that the Holy Spirit offers everyone the possibility of sharing in the Paschal Mystery in a manner known to God." Certainly, one cannot mistake the Pope's assertion that God's loving plan for salvation includes each and every person!

Evangelization as *"God's work"* (24) is clearly affirmed; it is based "not on human abilities but on the power of the Risen Lord" (23). Missionaries are conscious that they owe their faith and vocations "not to their own merits but to Christ's special grace" (11). They must believe that "it is not we who are the principal agents of the Church's mission, but Jesus Christ and his Spirit" (36). A missioner's faith journey "proceeds along *the path* already trodden by the Virgin Mary" (92).

Fifteen years earlier (1975) Paul VI wrote that "Modern man listens more willingly to witnesses than to teachers, and if he does listen to teachers, it is because they are witnesses" (EN 41). This passage is recalled in *Redemptoris Missio* (42). It must continue to remain a central focus if the Church wishes to respond "with generosity and holiness to the calls and challenges of our time" (92).

III. Synthetic Overview of Integral Evangelization

Without doubt, both Paul VI and John Paul II have gifted the Church with a rich understanding of the theology and praxis of evangelization. In presenting the vision of each pope, this piece has consciously limited itself to the one pivotal document on mission and evangelization authored by each pope. *Evangelii Nuntiandi* for Paul VI and *Redemptoris Missio* for John Paul II are each a microcosm of their understanding of missionary evangelization. This fact is borne out if one simply recalls the many facets of evangelization presented in each of the two previous sections. Can the discussion be taken further?

Additional insight can be drawn from two documents issued by the Secretariat for Non-Christians (founded in 1964 by Paul VI and renamed in 1988 the Pontifical Council for Interreligious Dialogue). On Pentecost Sunday, 1984, the Secretariat promulgated the document entitled: "The Attitude of the Church toward the Followers of Other Religions: Reflections and Orientations on Dialogue and Mission" (DM). Hidden in this little-known work on the interrelationship between dialogue and mission is a pivotal statement. This source affirms that mission and evangelization are understood "in the consciousness of the Church as a single but complex and articulated reality" (13).

Later, on Pentecost Sunday, 1991, the Pontifical Council for Interreligious Dialogue in conjunction with the Congregation for the Evangelization of Peoples presented the document: "Dialogue and Proclamation: Reflections and Orientations on Interreligious Dialogue and the Proclamation of the Gospel of Jesus Christ." Once again, the evangelizing mission of the Church is understood as a "single but complex and articulated reality" (2).

Both documents emphasize the unity and integral nature of evangelization, while at the same time affirming that evangelization necessarily comprises many dimensions; it is a complex reality. In addition, this multi-faceted concept can be explained and articulated.

NAMING THE ELEMENTS. Despite the lengthy and complex titles of the 1984 and 1991 documents just mentioned, these two sources have added considerable clarity to a Catholic understanding of missionary evangelization. The clarity results from the fact that "principal elements" are specifically named. Thus, mission and evangelization are composed of: **(a)** presence and witness; **(b)** commitment to social development and human liberation; **(c)** liturgical life, prayer and contemplation; **(d)** interreligious dialogue; and, **(e)** proclamation and catechesis (cf. DM 13 and DP 2). In a word, the one evangelizing mission of the Church is comprised of several component elements and authentic forms. This is integral or holistic evangelization; this is—in compact expression—the wide view of evangelization promoted by Paul VI and John Paul II in EN and RM.

This five-point vision has served the Church well over the past decade; this approach takes the thought of two popes and two documents and expresses it in a manner that ordinary Catholics can readily grasp and appreciate. At the same time, it does not do violence to the richness and complexity of missionary evangelization. One easily perceives that the thought expressed in EN and RM is adequately captured in this five-point schema; in turn, employing this helpful schema enables a smooth maneuvering through lengthy papal documents. Viewing evangelization through its various essential dimensions results in clarity, insight, and proper integration. This is a Catholic vision of evangelization.

EXPLORING THE FIVE DIMENSIONS. Further insight into the integral nature of evangelization is attained by specifically relating the five principal elements with both papal documents (EN and RM). This exercise illustrates that "evangelizing means bringing the Good News into all strata of humanity" (EN 18).

According to Paul VI, *Christian presence and witness of life* form the "initial act of evangelization" (EN 21). Daily activities, living together in harmony, lives as individuals of integrity, duties in the community—all these are to be a basic "faith-witness" that demonstrates how Christian living is shaped by Christian faith and values. Through this wordless witness, "Christians stir up irresistible questions in the hearts of those who see how they live" (EN 21). And, in today's world, people desire and respect authentic witnesses (cf. EN 41; RM 11, 42). In Asia, the late Mother Teresa of Calcutta, known for her loving and selfless care of the poorest of the poor, is an "icon" of Christian presence, life, and service.

Community living as good neighbors based on faith convictions should naturally issue in a *commitment to social development and human liberation*, a genuine service of humanity. This means serving the most unfortunate, witnessing to justice, defending the integrity of creation; this dimension of evangelization includes the whole area of social concerns, ranging from peace-building, education and health services to promoting family life and good government. The area of human development or human promotion is a vast area of the Church's evangelizing mission (cf. EN 18-19, 29-33; RM 58-60).

Integral evangelization and liberation will necessarily include *liturgical life, prayer and contemplation*. No one can effectively be engaged in the Church's mission without a strong faith and prayer-life. Evangelization needs holy men and women who are themselves on fire with the love of Christ; spreading the fire of the Gospel will be accomplished only by those already burning with an experience of Christ. Holiness is an irreplaceable condition for evangelizers. The "God-experience" achieved in prayer and contemplation, in sacramental and liturgical life, will illumine and transform all other dimensions of evangelization (cf. EN 23, 43-44, 47; RM 46-49, 87-92).

All evangelizing activities are inserted into specific contexts; particularly in Asia, these activities naturally assume an interreligious dimension. Thus, the Church in Asia, similar to most places in the world of today, accomplishes her mission in pluralistic and diverse cultures; she enters into *interreligious dialogue*, cooperating with the followers of the great religious traditions. Interreligious dialogue takes many forms; there are the dialogues of daily life, deeds of service, religious experts, and faith experience, as well as other forms. John Paul II asserts: "Interreligious dialogue is a part of the Church's evangelizing mission" (RM 55). This dialogue emerges from one's faith convictions. In contemporary circumstances, dialogue with religions and cultures is the truly appropriate Christian response (cf. EN 20, 53; RM 52-54, 55-57).

Finally, in mission today there is the role of *explicit Gospel proclamation and catechesis*. This dimension of evangelization includes preaching, catechesis on Christian life, teaching the content of the faith; in a word, this means "telling the Jesus story." When the Holy Spirit opens the door and when the time is opportune, Christians do tell the Jesus story, giving explicit witness and testimony to the faith. Others are invited, in freedom of conscience, to come to know, love and follow Jesus. Through proclamation Christians themselves are further instructed in their faith; this is the process through which the Christian faith is communicated to the next generation of believers (cf. EN 22, 27, 42; RM 44-51).

Obviously, these five dimensions of an integral understanding of evangelization complement and reinforce each other. In speaking of the complexity of the Church's evangelizing action, Paul VI gave a timely admonition: "Any partial and fragmentary definition which attempts to render the reality of evangelization in all its richness, complexity and dynamism does so only at the risk of impoverishing it and even of distorting it." The pope continued: "It is impossible to grasp the concept of evangelization unless one tries to keep in view all its essential elements" (EN 17).

Thus, an older concept of the Church's mission has been set aside. No longer are the elements of social justice, interfaith dialogue, peace-building, education and health care, life-witness, etc. simply "preparatory" to evangelization [*praeparatio evangelica*]; all five "principal elements" are constitutive of a holistic and integral understanding. Paul VI and John Paul II have expanded the horizons of evangelization; the more restrictive view, which held that only explicit Gospel proclamation and sacramental life constituted mission, has been superceded.

Concomitant with this expanded vision of evangelization, one finds a renewed emphasis on the missionary nature of the *entire Church* (cf. AG 2). Every baptized member of the Church is an evangelizer, whether layperson, ordained, or religious. Previously, when evangelization was linked more exclusively with explicit Gospel proclamation and sacramental life, laity often found it difficult to appreciate how they were to be evangelizers. Today, Catholic evangelization engages the entire Church (from top to bottom; especially, all the local churches), all states of life (lay, religious, ordained, married, single), all apostolic activities and forms of witness (the five principal elements—and other aspects). Yes, the totality of Christian missionary evangelization embraces all these dimensions.

CONCLUSION. This lengthy piece has attempted a panoramic overview of a Catholic vision of evangelization. Through a presentation of the vision of Paul VI and John Paul II in EN and RM (Parts I and II), the bases for a renewed, holistic, and integral understanding of evangelization were established. Part III presented a focused synthesis, employing the five principal and constitutive elements of evangelization.

When many words have been uttered, when much ink has been spilt, when definitions and categories have been clarified, and when one more presentation has been completed, Catholic Christians must step back and radically affirm that: *All mission and evangelization is God's project. The Holy Spirit is always the principal agent of evangelization.* For evangelizers, missionaries, catechists, religious and lay alike, mission necessarily means trying to find out what God wills and what he is doing. Then, authentic evangelizers bend their wills to God's will, joyfully surrender to God's loving plan, and expend all efforts and energy to become worthy instruments that enable God's design to unfold. Evangelization, at heart and center, is an issue of faith (cf. RM 11). For Christians, for all local Churches, to live is to evangelize!

* * *

SELECTED BIBLIOGRAPHY

RECENT POPES AND EVANGELIZATION

Almario, C., ed. *Evangelization in Asia.* Quezon City, Philippines: Claretian Publications, 1993.

Amaladoss, M. "Evangelization in Asia: A New Focus?" In *Making All Things New: Dialogue, Pluralism and Evangelization in Asia,* 103-120. Maryknoll, New York: Orbis Books, 1990.

Arévalo, C. **[A]** "The Church in Asia and Mission in the 1990s." FABC *Papers 57b.* Hong Kong: FABC Secretariat, 1990. **[B]** "Notes on the Apostolic Exhortation of Pope Paul VI, *Evangelii Nuntiandi.*" In *Faith, Ideologies and Christian Options* [Loyola Papers 7/8], ed. H. de la Costa et al., 38-60. Manila: Cardinal Bea Institute, 1976.

Bacani, T. **[A]** "The Need for a New Evangelization." In FABC *Papers 66:* 11-25. Hong Kong: FABC Secretariat, 1993. **[B]** "The Renewed Integral Evangelization Envisioned by the Second Plenary Council of the Philippines. *Philippiniana Sacra* 28/83 (May-August, 1993): 311-320.

Burrows, W., ed. *Redemption and Dialogue: Reading Redemptoris Missio and Dialogue and Proclamation.* Maryknoll, New York: Orbis Books, 1993.

Chandrakanthan, A. "Asian Bishops' Approaches to Evangelisation: A Theological Evaluation and Critique of the Statements of the Plenary Assemblies of the FABC (1970-1983)." *Indian Missiological Review* 9/2 (April, 1987): 105-127.

Claver, F. "The Church in Asia: Twenty Years after Vatican II." *East Asian Pastoral Review* 22/4 (1985): 316-323.

Degrijse, O. "John Paul II's Missionary Encyclical *Redemptoris Missio*: A Challenge for Missionary Institutes?" *Omnis Terra* 27/235 (February, 1993): 69-77 and 27/236 (March, 1993): 120-124.

Dorr, D. "*Redemptoris Missio*—Reflections on the Encyclical." *The Furrow* 42/6 (June, 1991): 339-347.

D'Souza, H. **[A]** "Pope John Paul II's New Challenge to Asia," *L'Osservatore Romano* 24/14 (April 8, 1991): 6, 8. **[B]** "*Redemptoris Missio* Confirms FABC Statements." *Asia Focus* 8/26 (July 10, 1992): 7.

Dulles, A. **[A]** "John Paul II and the New Evangelization." *America* 166/3 (February 1, 1992): 52-59, 69-72. **[B]** "Seven Essentials of Evangelization." *Origins* 25/23 (November 23, 1995): 397-400.

Dupuis, J. **[A]** "Apostolic Exhortation *Evangelii Nuntiandi* of Pope Paul VI." *Vidyajyoti* 40/5 (May, 1976): 218-230. **[B]** "FABC Focus on the Church's Evangelizing Mission in Asia Today." *Vidyajyoti* 56/9 (September, 1992): 449-468. **[C]** "Evangelization and Mission" In *Dictionary of Fundamental Theology*, ed. R. Latourelle, 275-282. New York: Crossroad, 1995.

Falciola, P. *Evangelization According to the Mind of Paul VI*. Rome: Pontifical Missionary Union, 1982.

Fitzgerald, M. "*Evangelii Nuntiandi* and World Religions." *African Ecclesial Review* 21/1 (February, 1979): 34-43.

Flannery, A., ed. *Evangelization Today*. Northport, New York: Costello Publishing Company, 1977.

Gabriel, M. *John Paul II's Mission Theology in Asia: Agenda for the Third Millennium* (2d ed.). Mandaluyong City, Philippines: Academic Publishing Corporation, 1999 [Extensive Bibliography].

George, F. "One Lord and One Church for One World: The Tenth Anniversary of *Redemptoris Missio*." *L'Osservatore Romano* 34/5 (January 31, 2001): 7-10.

Giordano, P. "Towards Understanding the New or Integral Evangelization: The Visit of Pope John Paul II to the Philippines, January 12-16, 1995." *Timon* 2 (1994-1995): 1-18.

Greinacher, N. and A. Müller, ed. *Evangelization in the World Today.* New York: The Seabury Press, 1979.

John Paul II. *Redemptoris Missio.* In *The Pope Speaks* 36/2 (1991): 138-183 [Synthesis Text: "Pope John Paul II's Gift." In *Living Mission: Challenges in Evangelization Today*, J. Kroeger, 141-159. Maryknoll, New York: Orbis Books and Quezon City, Philippines: Claretian Publications, 1994].

Karotemprel, S. **[A]** "*Redemptoris Missio* and Evangelization in Asia." *Indian Missiological Review* 14/3-4 (December, 1992): 28-33. **[B]** ed. *Following Christ in Mission: A Foundational Course in Missiology.* Pasay City, Philippines and Boston, Massachusetts: Paulines Publications, 1996.

Keerankeri, G. "Many Expressions of One Mission." *Vidyajyoti* 57/3 (February, 1993): 128-132.

Kroeger, J. **[A]** *The Philippine Church and Evangelization: 1965-1984* [*Human Promotion as an Integral Dimension of the Church's Mission of Evangelization: A Philippine Experience and Perspective since Vatican II — 1965-1984*]. Rome: Pontifical Gregorian University, 1985 [Extensive Bibliography]. **[B]** "Contemporary Mission in Asia." *The Japan Missionary Bulletin* 44/4 (Winter, 1990): 282-286. **[C]** "Rekindling Mission Vitality and Enthusiasm: *Redemptoris Missio*—A Commentary." *Indian Missiological Review* 14/3-4 (December, 1992): 15-22. **[D]** *Living Mission: Challenges in Evangelization Today.* Maryknoll, New York: Orbis Books and Manila, Philippines: Claretian Publications, 1994. **[E]** "*Redemptoris Missio.*" In *The Wojtyla Years* [*New Catholic Encyclopedia XX*], ed. J. Komonchak et al., 231-232. Washington, D.C.: The Catholic University of America, 2001.

Legaspi, L. "Integral Evangelization: Before/After PCP II—The Task Ahead." Keynote Address at the Mindanao-Sulu

Pastoral Conference (MSPC) VIII, Tagum, Davao del Norte, Philippines, October 28, 1992 [Photocopied Manuscript].

Lopez-Gay, J. "Theological Aspects of the Apostolic Exhortation *Evangelii Nuntiandi*," *Omnis Terra* 11/82 (February, 1977): 167-179.

McCormack, W., ed. *"To the Ends of the Earth":* Missionary *Catechesis of Pope John Paul* II. New York: Propagation of the Faith Publications, 1995.

McGregor, B. "Commentary on *Evangelii Nuntiandi.*" *Doctrine and Life* 27/3-4 (March-April, 1977): 53-97.

Miller, J., "Redemptoris Missio." In *The Encyclicals of John Paul* II, 478-570. Huntington, Indiana: Our Sunday Visitor, Inc., 1996 [Extensive Bibliography].

Müller, K. et al., ed. *Dictionary of Mission: Theology, History, Perspectives.* Maryknoll, New York: Orbis Books, 1997.

Neuner, J. "Mission in *Ad Gentes* and in *Redemptoris Missio.*" *Vidyajyoti* 56/5 (May, 1992): 228-241.

Paul VI. *Evangelii Nuntiandi.* In *The Pope Speaks* 21/1 (1976): 4-51 [Synthesis Text: "Pope Paul VI's Gift." In *Living Mission: Challenges in Evangelization Today*, J. Kroeger, 129-140. Maryknoll, New York: Orbis Books and Quezon City, Philippines: Claretian Publications, 1994].

Phan, P., ed. *The Asian Synod: Texts and Commentaries.* Maryknoll, New York: Orbis Books, 2002.

Piryns, E. "A New Approach to Mission and Evangelization." *Philippiniana Sacra* 30/88 (January-April, 1995): 81-98.

Quatra, M. *At the Side of the Multitudes.* Quezon City, Philippines: Claretian Publications, 2000.

Tan Yun-ka, J. *"Missio ad Gentes" in Asia: A Comparative Study of the Missiology of John Paul II and the Federation of Asian Bishops' Conferences.* Doctoral Thesis in Theology, Washington, D.C.: The Catholic University of America, 2002.

Ueffing, M. "A New Age in Mission." *Diwa* 19/2 (November, 1994): 131-138.

Vadakumpadan, P. *Evangelisation Today.* Shillong, India: Vendrame Missiological Institute [Sacred Heart College], 1989.

4

A CHURCH WALKING IN DIALOGUE

Interreligious Dialogue Milestones

Addressing the entire Church "at the beginning of the new millennium" which opens "a new stage of the Church's journey," Pope John Paul II presented pivotal areas of Church life requiring that she "take up her evangelizing mission with fresh enthusiasm" (1, 2). The purpose of the pope's *Novo Millennio Ineunte* (January 6, 2001) focused on enabling the Church to "shine ever more brightly in the variety of her gifts and in her unity as she journeys on" (3).

The pope addresses more than three dozen individual subject areas in this apostolic letter. Most themes are discussed rather briefly; however, five topics receive more lengthy treatment—extending to three numbered sections. Interreligious Dialogue is addressed in sections 54-56 under the heading "Dialogue and Mission." This comparatively lengthy treatment appears to emphasize the importance the pope allots to dialogue in the Church's mission of integral evangelization.

John Paul II asks the faithful to consider "the great challenge of interreligious dialogue to which we shall still be committed in the new millennium, in fidelity to the teachings of the Second Vatican Council.... This dialogue must continue.... [it] will be especially important in establishing a sure basis for peace.... The name of the one God must become increasingly what it is: a name of peace and a summons to peace" (55). This pope has clearly renewed the Church's mandate to sincerely engage in dialogue in fulfillment of her missionary vocation.

LOCAL CHURCH COMMITMENT. The Church in the Philippines, in her discussions and documents connected with the Jubilee Year and Church Renewal, reemphasized the importance of interreligious dialogue. Two sources illustrate this fact; they are: **(a)** the Pastoral Letter of the Catholic Bishops' Conference of the Philippines (July 5, 2000) entitled: "'Missions' and the Church in the Philippines"; and, **(b)** the Message of the National Pastoral Consultation on Church Renewal (January 27, 2001) entitled: "Behold I Make All Things New."

The Philippine bishops' "Mission Letter" notes: "Mission in Asia will call for new consciousness and knowledge regarding other religious traditions here in this continent in which almost all the great religions of humanity have been born. One of the 'new things' of mission in Asia will be the demand for a deepened understanding of other religious communities (specially the Islamic), their religiosity and their theologies. Attitudes of genuine respect and reverence for others' beliefs and spiritualities must precede and accompany all interreligious dialogue and all mission" (IV, 6).

The January 2001 consultation on Church Renewal stated: "We shall undertake our renewal efforts in fidelity to Jesus' will for unity among believers. Rooted in Christ, we shall strive to eradicate prejudices and to grow in deeper understanding and appreciation of other ecclesial communities and religious traditions, especially the followers of Islam. We shall engage in a dialogue of life, faith, prayer and common action with them. As a way to healing, reconciliation and national unity, we shall encourage dialogue among all sectors of society" (7-H).

SIGNPOSTS ALONG THE DIALOGUE ROAD. The renewed dialogue commitment by the local Church at the turn of the new millennium has an important history that is worthy of a brief examination. The Church would never have arrived at its present appreciation of dialogue without the innovations begun by Pope John XXIII; in his call for *aggiornamento* and his convocation of the Second Vatican Council he envisioned a wide and encompassing renewal of the whole Church. Today, from the vantage point of nearly four decades of experience after the close of Vatican II in 1965, a keen observer can readily identify the "path of dialogue" along which the Spirit has led Christians; local Churches can readily discern a "mandate for dialogue" in recent Church experience and reflection.

The Church's forty-year journey on the dialogue road reveals key milestones where growth and understanding have been achieved. Each milestone noted in this essay contains a brief description of the event itself, the progress it contributed, and the paths it noted for future growth in dialogue. On the one hand, the Church's milestones or signposts have been clear and encouraging; however, on the other hand, the general Church membership has been a reluctant pilgrim in walking the dialogue road. This succinct overview of significant milestones aims to encourage a fuller integration of dialogue within the Church's mission and ministry, an objective that both recent popes and local Churches have consistently promoted.

I. Secretariat for Non-Christians. On Pentecost (May 17) 1964, in the climate of the Second Vatican Council, Pope Paul VI instituted the Secretariat for Non-

Christians as an entity distinct from the Sacred Congregation for the Evangelization of Peoples. Renamed the Pontifical Council for Interreligious Dialogue in 1988, it was to serve as an institutional sign and structure of the Church's desire to meet and relate to the followers of other religious traditions of the world. Its task, as noted by Paul VI, was "to search for methods and ways of opening a suitable dialogue with non-Christians ... in order that non-Christians come to be known honestly and esteemed justly by Christians, and that in their turn non-Christians can adequately know and esteem Christian doctrine and life."

II. Encyclical: *Ecclesiam Suam*. Pope Paul VI published his programmatic encyclical letter *Ecclesiam Suam* on August 6, 1964 (between the second and third sessions of Vatican II). This *"magna carta* of dialogue" introduces the term "dialogue"; this is the first time that the term is used in an encyclical (over half of the document is devoted to a discussion of the need, source, characteristics, modes, partners, challenges and goals of dialogue): "The Church should enter into dialogue with the world in which it exists and labors" (67). "The dialogue of salvation was opened spontaneously on the initiative of God: He [God] loved us first" (74). We "need to wait for the hour when God may make our dialogue effective" (79).

"Dialogue is, then, a method of accomplishing the apostolic mission" (83). "The Church is not unaware of the formidable dimensions of such a mission" (99). It is also directed towards "the followers of the great Afro-Asiatic religions" (111). We "recognize and respect the moral and spiritual values of various non-Christian religions, and we desire to join with them in promoting and defending common ideals of religious liberty, human brotherhood, good culture, social welfare and civil order" (112).

III. Second Vatican Council. Five documents of Vatican II contain important elements for understanding the Church's role vis-a-vis world religions (*Nostra Aetate, Lumen Gentium, Ad Gentes, Gaudium et Spes,* and *Dignitatis Humanae*). Some general themes are: the need to recognize within religions "elements of truth and grace" (AG 9), "treasures which the bountiful God has distributed among the nations of the earth" (AG 11), "a ray of that Truth which enlightens all men" (NA 2); recognition of the work of the Holy Spirit (GS 11; AG 4); the presence of treasures of the ascetical and contemplative life (AG 15, 18) and the presence of "Seeds of the Word" (LG 17; AG 11).

The Council promotes an attitude of profound respect toward all world religions (AG 10), specifically primitive and traditional religions (NA 2), Hinduism (NA 2), Buddhism (NA 2), Islam (NA 3; LG 16), and Judaism (NA 4; LG 16). It encourages dialogue and collaboration (NA 2); it is through dialogue that Christians can "receive the inspirations of the Spirit and follow them ardently" (GS 92). The Council challenges all Christians: "we are obliged to hold that the Holy Spirit offers everyone the possibility of sharing in the Paschal Mystery in a manner known to God" (GS 22).

IV. FABC First Plenary Assembly. The Federation of Asian Bishops' Conferences (FABC) met in Taipei, Taiwan (April 22-27, 1974) to prepare for the international Synod on Evangelization. Their landmark document *Evangelization in Modern Day Asia* spoke of "the integral preaching of the Gospel" (23), "the building up of a truly local church" (9) and the triple dialogue with peoples, cultures, and religions (12). The Church in Asia especially needs to engage in "a dialogue with the great religious traditions of our peoples" (13), which are "significant and positive elements in the economy of God's design of salvation" (14); "they have been the treasury of the religious experience of our ancestors" (14). "And how can we not acknowledge that God has drawn our peoples to Himself through them?" (15). FABC recommended the need to "evolve a working concept of evangelization that embraces, as integral to that concept, genuine dialogue with the great living religions of Asia" (3a).

V. Synod on Evangelization of the Modern World. The short declaration at the end of the 1974 Synod proclaimed: "Confident in the action of the Holy Spirit which overflows the bounds of the Christian community, we wish to foster dialogue with non-Christian religions, so that we may reach a better understanding of the gospel's newness and of the fullness of revelation, and thus may be in a better position to show to others how the salvific truth of God's love is fulfilled in Christ" (11).

VI. Apostolic Exhortation: *Evangelii Nuntiandi*. One year after the Synod Paul VI published *Evangelii Nuntiandi* (December 8, 1975). Evangelization is seen as the "vocation proper to the Church, her deepest identity. She exists in order to evangelize" (14). The understanding of evangelization in EN is a broad one: "evangelizing means bringing the Good News into all the strata of humanity" (18). "Any partial and fragmentary definition which attempts to render the reality of evangelization in all its richness, complexity and dynamism does so only at the risk of impoverishing it and even of distorting it. It is impossible to grasp the concept of evangelization unless one tries to keep in view all of its essential elements" (17).

EN speaks of the Church's esteem and respect for non-Christian religions (53) because "they are the living expression of the soul of vast groups of people ... they have taught generations of people how to pray ... they are all impregnated with innumerable 'seeds of the Word' and can constitute a true 'preparation for the Gospel'."

The Church needs "to offer to the missionaries of today and of tomorrow new horizons in their contacts with non-Christian religions" (53).

VII. Dialogue and Mission. On Pentecost (June 10) 1984, the twentieth anniversary of the creation of the Secretariat for Non-Christians, the Church published "The Attitude of the Church towards the Followers of Other Religions: Reflections and Orientations on Dialogue and Mission." Approved by the pope, the document expressly places interreligious dialogue within the purview of the Church's evangelizing mission: "dialogue finds its place within the Church's salvific mission; for this reason it is a dialogue of salvation" (John Paul II: Introduction, 5; cf. *Ecclesiam Suam* 74).

The document gives interreligious dialogue a broad definition: "It means not only discussion, but also includes all positive and constructive interreligious relations with individuals and communities of other faiths which are directed at mutual understanding and enrichment" (3). Its main concern is "the relationship which exists between dialogue and mission" (5). The document presents the five dimensions of integral mission / evangelization and notes how they are understood "in the consciousness of the church as a single but complex and articulated reality" (13). Both local Churches and missionaries are "responsible for the totality of mission" (14), because "Christian mission embraces all these elements" (13). Four forms of dialogue are presented in detail (25-35).

VIII. World Day of Prayer for Peace at Assisi. In the context of the International Year of Peace, on October 27, 1986, John Paul II invited representatives of other Christian Churches and Ecclesial Communities and of the major World Religions to come on pilgrimage to Assisi to pray and fast for world peace. Explaining the event, John Paul II noted: "The event of Assisi can be considered as a visible illustration, a concrete example, a catechesis, intelligible to all, of what is presupposed and signified by the commitment to ecumenism and to interreligious dialogue which was recommended and promoted by the Second Vatican Council" (7). He added: "Either we learn to walk together in peace and harmony, or we drift apart and ruin ourselves and others" (5).

IX. Theses on Interreligious Dialogue (FABC). In April 1987, after two years of study and consultation by the Federation of Asian Bishops' Conferences (FABC) Theological Advisory Commission (TAC), the document *Theses on Interreligious Dialogue: An Essay in Pastoral Theological Reflection* was released. The aim of the document was to "facilitate a new insight into the identity of the Church in a religiously pluralistic world and a renewal of its mission" (0.9). The document presents a comprehensive vision of interfaith dialogue in seven closely reasoned theses with extensive commentary. They address important theological-missiological questions, consistently asserting that dialogue "is an integral dimension of the mission of the Church, which is the sacrament of the Kingdom of God proclaimed by Jesus" (Thesis 2). This document is illustrative of the holistic FABC vision that consistently identifies dialogue as the "distinctive mode" of mission in the Asian continent (FABC V: 4.1).

X. Encyclical: *Redemptoris Missio*. John Paul II's mission encyclical, dated December 7, 1990, addresses the "Permanent Validity of the Church's Missionary Mandate." Within the fourth chapter "The Paths of Mission" a specific section addresses "Dialogue with our Brothers and Sisters of Other Religions" (55-57). It is an exceedingly rich section: "Interreligious dialogue is a part of the Church's evangelizing mission; ... dialogue is not in opposition to mission *ad gentes*; indeed, it has special links with that mission and is one of its expressions; ... the Church sees no conflict between proclaiming Christ and engaging in interreligious dialogue" (55). "Each member of the faithful and all Christian communities are called to practice dialogue.... I [John Paul II] am well aware that many missionaries and Christian communities find in the difficult and often misunderstood path of dialogue their only way of bearing sincere witness to Christ and offering generous service to others. I wish to encourage them..." (57).

XI. *Dialogue and Proclamation.* On Pentecost (May 19) 1991 the Pontifical Council for Interreligious Dialogue and the Congregation for the Evangelization of Peoples jointly issued "Dialogue and Proclamation: Reflections and Orientations on Interreligious Dialogue and the Proclamation of the Gospel of Jesus Christ." The document explicitly affirms the holistic and integral nature of the evangelization process and mentions five principal elements of mission (2). Discussing "the relationship between dialogue and proclamation" (4), the document quotes John Paul II: "Just as interreligious dialogue is one element in the mission of the Church, the proclamation of God's saving work in Our Lord Jesus Christ is another.... There can be no question of choosing one and ignoring or rejecting the other" (6). "Both are legitimate and necessary" (77).

There are many "signs of the times" (social, cultural, religious and political) and a *religious* sensitivity and attentiveness is an important avenue to hear "the Spirit of God [who] is speaking, teaching, and guiding" (78). "All Christians are called to be personally involved in these two ways of carrying out the one mission of the Church, namely proclamation and dialogue" (82). "Yet more than tasks to be accomplished, dialogue and proclamation are graces to be sought in prayer" (89).

XII.   Continental Synods and Apostolic Exhortations. As part of the celebration of the Jubilee Year 2000, John Paul II convoked a series of continental synods. In those areas of the world where a variety of religious traditions are found and form an integral dimension of people's indigenous culture and faith, interreligious dialogue necessarily became a key dimension in understanding the Church's presence and ministry.

On the Feast of the Triumph of the Holy Cross (September 14) 1995, John Paul II released the Post-Synodal Apostolic Exhortation, *Ecclesia in Africa*. In reference to dialogue (65-67), the document notes: "Commitment to dialogue must also embrace all Muslims of good will" (66). "With regard to African traditional religion, a serene and prudent dialogue will be able ... to foster the assimilation of positive values.... They can be seen as a *preparation for the Gospel*.... The adherents of African traditional religion should therefore be treated with great respect and esteem, and all inaccurate and disrespectful language should be avoided" (67). This is a task given to the Church in Africa in fulfillment of "her evangelizing mission towards the year 2000" (8).

The Church in Asia (home to more than 85% of the world's non-Christians) celebrated the "Asian Synod" in 1998; the final apostolic exhortation *Ecclesia in Asia* was released on November 6, 1999 during a pastoral visit of John Paul II to India. As expected, one finds rich insights into dialogue in this document (29-31): "From the Christian point of view, interreligious dialogue is more than a way of fostering mutual knowledge and enrichment; it is a part of the Church's evangelizing mission, an expression of the mission *ad gentes*.... It is therefore important for the Church in Asia to provide suitable models of interreligious dialogue—evangelization in dialogue and dialogue for evangelization—and suitable training for those involved.... Communion and dialogue are two essential aspects of the Church's mission.... Only if the People of God recognize the gift that is theirs in Christ will they be able to communicate that gift to others through *proclamation* and *dialogue*" (31).

XIII. PCID Religious Forum and Assisi Day of Prayer for Peace. On November 18, 2001 during his Angelus Prayer, Pope John Paul II announced another Church endeavor to promote dialogue and peace: "I wish to announce that I intend to invite representatives of the religions of the world to come to Assisi on 24th January 2002 to pray for the end of conflict and the promotion of true peace, and to come together, especially Christians and Muslims, to declare before the world that religion must never become a source of conflict, hatred and violence." Seizing this opportunity when so many religious leaders would gather, the Pontifical Council for Interreligious Dialogue (PCID) organized a "Forum on the Contribution of Religions for the Cause of Peace" on January 23, 2002 in the Vatican. Thus, a two-day event unfolded during which eminent religious leaders appealed for peace in the world and committed themselves to work together to heal the wounds of humanity.

The Day of Prayer for Peace in Assisi on January 24, 2002 proved to be another landmark in the religious history of humankind. When the Holy Father addressed the assembly, he spoke of two "pillars" of peace, namely, commitment to *justice* and readiness to *forgive*. The pope said: "*Justice*, first of all, because there can be no true peace without respect for the dignity of persons and peoples, respect for the rights and duties of each person and respect for an equal distribution of benefits and burdens between individuals and in society as a whole. It can never be forgotten that situations of oppression and exclusion are often at the source of violence and terrorism. But *forgiveness* too, because human justice is subject to frailty and to the pressures of individual and group egoism. Forgiveness alone heals the wounds of the heart and fully restores damaged human relations."

The religious leaders who gathered in Assisi forged and signed a powerfully worded ten-point "Common Commitment to Peace." The first statement captures the tone and spirit of the document: "We commit ourselves to proclaiming our firm conviction that violence and terrorism are incompatible with the authentic spirit of religion, and, as we condemn every recourse to violence and war in the name of God or religion, we commit ourselves to doing everything possible to eliminate the root causes of terrorism." With evident emotion, John Paul II concluded the Assisi event with these words: "Violence never again! War never again! Terrorism never again! In the name of God, may every religion bring upon the earth: Justice and Peace, Forgiveness and Life, Love!"

POPE JOHN PAUL II. This essay opened with a citation from the pope's programmatic apostolic letter *Novo Millennio Ineunte*, where he affirms the importance of interfaith dialogue in the new millennium; he views commitment to dialogue as an imperative demanded of all local Churches: "It is our task to follow with great fidelity the Council's teaching and the path which it has traced" (56).

Commitment to the promotion of dialogue is one hallmark of his pontificate, now extending well over two decades. He repeatedly emphasizes the role that dialogue plays within the evangelizing mission of the

Church; in his missionary journeys he constantly seeks opportunities to respectfully interact with the followers of various religions and faith traditions. From his voluminous statements on the panorama of interreligious themes, some representative quotes—in addition to those already presented—manifest the variety of his unique insights.

"Christians will, moreover, join hands with all men and women of good will [and] work together in order to bring about a more just and peaceful society in which the poor will be the first to be served" (Manila, Philippines; February 21, 1981).

"Christians and Muslims, in general, have badly understood each other, and sometimes, in the past, we have opposed and even exhausted each other in polemics and in wars. I believe that today, God invites us *to change our old practices*. We must respect each other, and also we must stimulate each other in good works on the path of God" (Casablanca, Morocco; August 19, 1985).

"By dialogue we let God be present in our midst, for as we open ourselves to one another, we open ourselves to God" (Madras, India; February 5, 1986).

"Interreligious dialogue is 'a Christian work desired by God' and 'one element in the *mission of the Church*'; the commitment of the Catholic Church to dialogue with the followers of other religions remains firm and unchanged" (Rome, Italy; April 28, 1987).

"Throughout my Pontificate it has been my constant concern to fulfill the apostolic and pastoral task of both dialogue and proclamation. On my last visit to Africa, I met leaders of African traditional religions and witnessed their awareness of God's nearness and their appreciation of the ethical values of a godly person" (Rome, Italy; April 28, 1987).

"Respectful dialogue with others also enables us to be enriched by their insights, challenged by their questions, and impelled to deepen our knowledge of the truth. Far from stifling dialogue or rendering it superfluous, *a commitment to the truth of one's religious tradition* by its very nature *makes dialogue with others both necessary and fruitful*" (Jakarta, Indonesia; October 10, 1989).

"Interreligious dialogue at its deepest level is always a *dialogue of salvation*, because it seeks to discover, clarify and understand better the signs of the age-long dialogue which God maintains with humanity" (Vatican City; November 13, 1992).

"It is a sign of hope that the religions of the world are becoming more aware of their shared responsibility for the well-being of the human family. This is a crucial part of *the globalization of solidarity* which must come if the future of the world is to be secure.... To choose tolerance, dialogue and cooperation as the path into the future is to preserve what is most precious in the great religious heritage of mankind" (New Delhi, India; November 7, 1999).

"I address today a *heartfelt appeal* to those lands experiencing the upheavals of conflict, which are bringing unspeakable suffering for their defenseless peoples. *Everyone must be committed to peace*. But it must be true peace, based on mutual respect, on the rejection of fundamentalism and every form of imperialism, on the pursuit of dialogue as the only effective means of resolving tensions, so that entire nations are saved from the cruelty of violence.... *No one has the right to call upon God to justify their own selfish interests.... I ask religious leaders to reject all violence as offensive to the name of God*, and to be tireless promoters of peace and harmony, with respect for the rights of one and all" (Baku, Azerbaijan; May 22, 2002).

CONCLUSION. This essay has attempted to manifest the clear "dialogue mandate" that the local Churches have received in the Vatican II era. It highlighted thirteen pivotal moments within the Vatican II era and added additional, pertinent citations from John Paul II. All this material portrays the Church's thought and direction vis-a-vis dialogue and evangelization—as she continues her pilgrim journey in a new millennium.

In addition, at the heart of recent Catholic literature on dialogue is an operative vision of evangelization that is broad, comprehensive, and holistic; it is often termed "integral evangelization." Several elements—including interreligious dialogue—are seen as constitutive dimensions of this evangelization process. The Church consistently affirms her commitment to "integral evangelization," realizing that evangelization culminates in the proclamation of the Good News of Jesus Christ— whenever, wherever, and however this is practically and respectfully possible.

Within integral and holistic evangelization, dialogue remains an essential and fundamental commitment—yes, a *mandate*—for the universal Church as well as for each and every local Church. In fulfilling her mission, the Church engages the followers of various faith traditions, because she believes that *in this encounter all dialogue partners will experience a mutual evangelization under the influence of the Holy Spirit.*

* * *

SELECTED BIBLIOGRAPHY

INTERRELIGIOUS DIALOGUE

Amaladoss, M. "Interreligious Dialogue: A View from Asia." *International Bulletin of Missionary Research* 19/1 (January, 1995): 2-5.

Arinze, F. **[A]** *The Church in Dialogue: Walking with Other Believers.* San Francisco: Ignatius Press, 1990. **[B]** *Meeting Other Believers.* Shillong, India: Vendrame Institute Publications, 1998. **[C]** "The Rich Religious Dimension of Tribal Religions." *Pro Dialogo* 99 (1998/3): 289-294. **[D]** "Interreligious Dialogue in the Third Millennium." *Studia Missionalia* 48 (1999): 203-213.

Borelli, J. "John Paul II and Interreligious Dialogue." In *The Wojtyla Years* [New Catholic Encyclopedia XX], ed. J. Komonchak et al., 81-88. Washington, D.C.: The Catholic University of America, 2001.

Bormans, M. *Guidelines for Dialogue between Christians and Muslims.* New York: Paulist Press, 1990.

Burrows, W., ed. *Redemption and Dialogue: Reading Redemptoris Missio and Dialogue and Proclamation.* Maryknoll, New York: Orbis Books, 1994.

Capalla, F. "Interreligious Dialogue Should Be Mandatory Subject." *L'Osservatore Romano* 31/18 (May 6, 1998): 4-5.

Chia, E., ed. *Dialogue? Resource Manual for Catholics in Asia.* Bangkok: FABC Office of Ecumenical and Interreligious Affairs, 2001.

Dabre, T. "The Church in Dialogue: Dialogue within the Church." *Pro Dialogo* 112 (2003/1): 85-95.

D'Ambra, S. "Interreligious Dialogue in *Ecclesia in Asia.*" In *The Future of the Asian Churches: The Asian Synod and Ecclesia in Asia,* ed. J. Kroeger and P. Phan, 110-114. Quezon City, Philippines: Claretian Publications, 2002.

D'Costa, G. **[A]** *Theology and Religious Pluralism: The Challenge of Other Religions.* Oxford: Basil Blackwell, 1986. **[B]** *Christian Uniqueness Reconsidered.* Maryknoll, New York: Orbis Books, 1990. **[C]** *The Meeting of Religions and the Trinity.* Maryknoll, New York: Orbis Books, 2000.

Degryse, O. *Interreligious Dialogue: The Asian Churches Set the Tone.* Louvain: Catholic University, 1999.

Dupuis, J. **[A]** *Jesus Christ at the Encounter of World Religions.* Maryknoll, New York: Orbis Books, 1991. **[B]** *Toward a Christian Theology of Religious Pluralism.* Maryknoll, New York: Orbis Books, 1997. **[C]** *Christ and the Religions: From Confrontation to Dialogue.* Maryknoll, New York: Orbis Books, 2002.

Evers, G., ed. *Bibliography on Interreligious Dialogue* [*Theology in Context Supplements* 7]. Aachen, Germany: Institute of Missiology, 1992.

FABC:TAC (Federation of Asian Bishops' Conferences: Theological Advisory Commission). "Theses on Interreligious Dialogue: An Essay in Pastoral Theological Reflection." In *Being Church in Asia,* ed. J. Gnanapiragasam and F. Wilfred, 7-28. Quezon City, Philippines: Claretian Publications, 1994 [See: FABC *Papers* 48: 1-22].

Fitzgerald, M. **[A]** "Other Religions in the Catechism of the Catholic Church." *Islamochristiana* 19 (1993): 29-41. **[B]** "The Spirituality of Interreligious Dialogue." *Origins* 28/36 (February 25, 1999): 631-633. **[C]** "Pope John Paul II and Interreligious Dialogue: A Catholic Assessment." In *John Paul II and Interreligious Dialogue,* ed.

B. Sherwin and H. Kasimov, 207-220. Maryknoll, New York: Orbis Books, 1999.

Gioia, F., ed. *Interreligious Dialogue: The Official Teaching of the Catholic Church* (1963-1995). Boston: Pauline Books and Media, 1997.

Hoechman, R. "What Is the Agenda of Interreligious Dialogue?" *Ecumenical Trends* 29/8 (September, 2000): 117-122.

ITC (International Theological Commission). "Christianity and World Religions." *Origins* 27/10 (August 14, 1997): 149, 151-166.

Jadot, J. "The Growth in Roman Catholic Commitment to Interreligious Dialogue since Vatican II." *Journal of Ecumenical Studies* 20/3 (Summer, 1983): 365-378.

John Paul II. [A] "The Meaning of the Assisi Day of Prayer." *Origins* 16/31 (January 15, 1987): 561-563. **[B]** "The Spirituality of Interreligious Dialogue." *Origins* 31/24 (November 22, 2001): 404-405.

Kasper, W. "Relating Christ's Universality to Interreligious Dialogue." *Origins* 30/21 (November 2, 2000): 321, 323-327.

Knitter, P. **[A]** *One Earth, Many Religions: Multifaith Dialogue and Global Responsibility.* Maryknoll, New York: Orbis Books, 1995. **[B]** *Jesus and the Other Names: Christian Mission and Global Responsibility.* Maryknoll, New York: Orbis Books, 1996. **[C]** *Introducing Theologies of Religions.* Maryknoll, New York: Orbis Books, 2002.

Kroeger, J. **[A]** "The Commitment of Mission Societies in Asia to Interreligious Dialogue." *East Asian Pastoral Review* 26/3-4 (1989): 266-275. **[B]** *Interreligious Dialogue: Catholic Perspectives.* Davao City, Philippines: Mission Studies Institute, 1990. **[C]** "Cruciform Dialogue in Mission." *Bulletin: Pontificium Consilium pro Dialogo Inter Religiones* 28/2 [83] (1993): 147-152. **[D]** "Bridging Interreligious Dialogue and Conversion." *Review for Religious* 55/1 (January-February, 1996): 46-54. **[E]** "Milestones in Interreligious Dialogue." *Review for Religious* 56/3 (May-June, 1997): 268-276.

Kung, H. **[A]** *Christianity and World Religions: Paths to Dialogue.* Maryknoll, New York: Orbis Books, 1986. **[B]** *Tracing the Way: Spiritual Dimensions of the World Religions.* New York: Continuum, 2002.

LaRousse, W. *Walking Together, Seeking Peace: The Local Church of Mindanao-Sulu Journeying in Dialogue with the Muslim Community* (1965-2000). Quezon City, Philippines: Claretian Publications, 2001 [Extensive Bibliography].

Michel, T. **[A]** "Interreligious Dialogue in the Context of the Asian Synod." In A *Church on the Threshold,* ed. M. Seigel, 3-14. Rome: SEDOS, 1998. **[B]** "A Variety of Approaches to Interfaith Dialogue." *Encounter: Documents for Muslim-Christian Understanding.* 249 (November, 1998): 3-9.

Painadath, S. "Theological Perspectives of FABC on Interreligious Dialogue." *Jeevadhara* 27/160 (July, 1997): 272-288.

Pandiappallil, J. *Jesus the Christ and Religious Pluralism.* New York: The Crossroad Publishing Company, 2001.

Paul VI. *Ecclesiam Suam. The Pope Speaks* 10/3 (1964-1965): 253-292.

PCID (Pontifical Council for Interreligious Dialogue). **[A]** "The Attitude of the Church Towards the Followers of Other Religions: Reflections and Orientations on Mission and Dialogue." *L'Osservatore Romano* 17/26 (June 25, 1984): 10-11. **[B]** "Dialogue and

Proclamation: Reflections and Orientations on Interreligious Dialogue and the Proclamation of the Gospel of Jesus Christ." Vatican City: PCID, 1991. **[C]** *Towards a Culture of Dialogue.* Vatican City: PCID, 1999. **[D]** *Meeting in Friendship.* Vatican City: PCID, 2000. **[E]** *Peace: A Single Goal and a Shared Intention.* Vatican City: PCID, 2002.

Pieris, A. "Interreligious Dialogue and Theology of Religions: An Asian Paradigm." In *Fire and Water: Basic Issues in Asian Buddhism and Christianity.* 154-161. Maryknoll, New York: Orbis Books, 1996.

Poulet-Mathis, A. "Ecumenical and Interreligious Dialogue in Asia." In *Mission and Dialogue: Theory and Practice,* ed. L. Mercado and J. Knight, 63-93. Manila: Divine Word Publications, 1989.

Schreiter, R. "Interreligious Dialogue: A Hundred Years On." *New Theology Review* 6/3 (August, 1993): 6-17.

Sherwin, B. and H. Kasimow, ed. *John Paul II and Interreligious Dialogue.* Maryknoll, New York: Orbis Books, 1999.

Swidler, L. **[A]** "The Dialogue Decalogue: Ground Rules for Interreligious Dialogue." *Horizons* 10/2 (Fall, 1983): 348-351. **[B]** "Interreligious Dialogue: A Christian Necessity." *Cross Currents* 35/2-3 (Summer-Fall, 1985): 129-147.

Thangaraj, M.T. *Relating to People of Other Religions: What Every Christian Needs to Know.* Nashville, Tennessee: Abingdon Press, 1997.

Wilfred, F. "Dialogue Gasping for Breath? Towards New Frontiers in Interreligious Dialogue." *FABC Papers* 49. Hong Kong: FABC Secretariat, 1987: 32-52.

Wolanin, A. "Dialogue and Proclamation." *Omnis Terra* [English Edition] 34/305 (March, 2000): 92-101.

World Council of Churches. "Guidelines for Dialogue and Relations with People of Other Religions." *Current Dialogue* 40 (December, 2002): 16-21.

Zago, M. **[A]** "Dialogue in the Mission of the Churches of Asia: Theological Basis and Pastoral Perspectives." *Kerygma* 17 (1983): 185-206. **[B]** "Interreligious Dialogue." In *Following Christ in Mission*, ed. S. Karotemprel et al., 101-109. Pasay City, Philippines: Paulines Publications, 1996. **[C]** "The Spirituality of Dialogue." *Pro Dialogo* 101 (1999/2): 233-247.

5

NAMING THE CONVERSION WE SEEK
Mission and Paschal Perspectives

Christian missionaries and evangelizers seek the "conversion" of the people they encounter and with whom they share their lives. However, in light of recent Christian and Catholic missionary experience and theological development, it is necessary to "name" or identify the type of conversion that is desired. What is the vision and goal that motivates Christian missionaries to go forth to the nations, to the ends of the earth? How do missionaries authentically respect people's freedom of conscience, their experience, their religions and cultures? And how, at the same time, do evangelizers in the local Church remain people of integrity who are committed to propagating their Christian faith? Treating the topic of "conversion" demands a carefully nuanced, updated, and holistic ecclesiology and missiology.

The theology of mission and conversion must be anchored in reality and is best approached in a concrete manner. Allow me to narrate the following experience which has helped shape my views on conversion and mission.

A BANGLADESHI BEGGAR. During the Lenten season some few years ago, while I was a visiting professor in Dhaka, Bangladesh, I had a "graced moment," a "defining experience" in my missionary awareness and perspective. It has remained seared in my consciousness and has forced me to ask many foundational questions about mission and my own commitment. It involves a Bangladeshi beggar woman.

I saw her on the road, in front of the large walled compound of a wealthy family dwelling. I could not clearly see her face, as she was several hundred feet ahead of me. Her tattered clothes covered a malnourished body; she was alone, although other beggars were walking ahead of her on the road. I was proceeding along the same path, leisurely taking a late afternoon walk.

Suddenly a luxury car approached with its horn blowing. The driver probably wanted the beggars to disperse and also wanted the gate of the compound opened by the servants. The woman appeared startled as the car turned sharply in front of her and the gate swung open. Within seconds two large dogs emerged from the compound and jumped at the woman, knocking her to the ground. She screamed and cried both from fear and the pain caused by the dogs nipping at her. I stood frozen, horrified at the sight.

A well-dressed madam promptly emerged from the chauffeur-driven car. She ordered the driver to bring the car into the compound; the dogs were called to return inside; the servants were commanded to close and lock the gate. And, the beggar woman? She was left alone on the ground—outside the gate (cf. Heb 13:12). I stood helpless, gazing at this appalling scene.

Only the other frightened beggars came to the aid of the woman. Only they showed mercy and compassion. I stood at a distance and wept at this scene of crucifixion. I admitted to being a guilty bystander. My fears and inadequacies left me paralyzed. I had not one *taka* coin in my pocket to give; I could not offer one word of consolation in the Bengali language which I did not speak; I did not approach the woman for fear of misinterpretation that a foreign man would touch a Bengali woman in public in this strictly Islamic culture. I simply wept in solidarity. I wept long and hard. And, in succeeding years, I have frequently returned to that scene and prayed to God: "Do not let me forget that experience. Allow it to shape my life and mission vision. Permit it to remain a 'defining moment' in understanding my mission vocation."

EMBRACING A BROKEN WORLD. This experience of the Bangladeshi beggar-woman has forced me to look closely at the large scale of suffering in the contemporary world. Often such human misery is reduced to cold statistics; still the numbers are staggering.

It has been noted that "40,000 children under the age of five die every day due to lack of basic vaccines that prevent childhood diseases; each day 500 million people go hungry; over one billion people live in extreme poverty; 40 million people die yearly of malnutrition and hunger; ... the list of such concrete sufferings and their devastating consequences goes on" (Tesfai 1).

My experience on the road in Dhaka, Bangladesh with the beggar-woman no longer allows me to view people as statistical abstractions or faceless victims. All Christians—all members of the local Church—are called to embrace the world and suffering humanity. Christians must recognize "the existence of a crucified people" and strive to "take them down from the cross" (Sobrino vii).

Suffering and the reality of a broken world are existentials of the human situation. No one escapes these common and universal realities; they are not borderline phenomena; they are at the center and depths of human existence. As Pope John Paul II notes: "The reality of suffering is ever before our eyes and often in the body, soul and heart of each of us" (LR 316).

The suffering that is inherent in human experience impacts the situation of the local Church as she concretely lives out her missionary calling. It affects one's view of mission praxis as well as mission theory. The traditional dialogue partner of mission theology has been the unbeliever; today the unbeliever / non-Christian still remains the dialogue partner; however, particular attention is focused on humanity's concrete experience of disaster, weakness, and suffering. Thus, human brokenness becomes a clear point of insertion for contemporary missiology. The local-Church-in-mission is to embrace suffering humanity, just as Christ "pitched his tent among us" through the incarnation.

John Paul II has noted that suffering is that "universal theme that accompanies humanity at every point" (SD 105) of human existence. "The Church has to try to meet humanity in a special way on the path of his suffering" (SD 106). Missionary by nature, each local Church must look squarely at the fundamental realities of the world today, allowing them to impinge upon her and disturb her in their naked reality. The Christian community must not join with those who fall into escapism and denial of the world's harsh realities.

HUMAN AND CHRISTIAN PERSPECTIVES. Humanity has a common origin and unity in its creator; it also is meant to be united in solidarity as it faces life's vicissitudes and sufferings. This mystery of human unity in the cycles of life and death is affirmed by Christian tradition; it is also a common theme in all the world's great religious traditions (cf. Fernando 23-29; Peiró 410-414; Tesfai 63-66).

All human life has a paschal configuration; its pattern continually moves through death to renewed life.

Life's paschal paradigm, universally shared by all people (although varying terminology may be used), sees people struggling to move through darkness to light, through captivity to freedom, through dryness to growth, through alienation to union, through suffering and brokenness to wholeness. Or again, life has an internal dynamic focused on the movement through death to life in all its dimensions; individuals and communities struggle to move "from falsehood to truth, from apathy to responsibility, from margination to participation, from loneliness and isolation to universal communion, from sin to grace" (Kroeger 1994, 57-58). Becoming a missionary local Church today demands an engagement with humanity's experience of life and death realities. Christians appreciate that paschal dimensions are characteristic of all life situations, and that they find an immediacy and poignancy in the reality of human brokenness and suffering.

Catholic theology asserts that the Spirit of God is present and active within the lives of all peoples—even in their experience of brokenness. God's grace is always present and operative. The Second Vatican Council forcefully stated that, as Christian believers, "we must hold that the Holy Spirit offers to all the possibility of being made partners, in a way known to God, in the Paschal mystery" (GS 22). This is the only quote that is used three times in the pope's mission encyclical *Redemptoris Missio* (RM 6, 10, 28). In his writings, John Paul II uses the phrase repeatedly; certainly, it is one of his guiding missiological principles.

This text of Vatican II affirms the action of the Holy Spirit in the hearts of all people. Christians believe that "the Spirit of God is constantly at work in ways that pass human understanding" (WCC 446). The universal work of the Spirit serves to enlighten people's experience of their paschal realities of dying and rising; life itself, including suffering, has the possibility of opening all peoples to experience God's salvation through the paschal mystery.

Note that GS 22 "declares unambiguously that there is only one way which leads to everlasting salvation, a way which is valid for Christians as well as non-Christians, and that is: association with the paschal mystery" (Moling 291). The redemptive grace of Christ is available for all who in their own way and even without knowing it obey the law of the paschal mystery and take it as a guiding norm for their consciences and lives. This astonishing assertion has important consequences regarding the approach to conversion that contemporary mission pursues.

The Christian faith is, at heart, a paschal faith. Thus, if all reality has a paschal paradigm and all life is shaped by rhythms of life through death, then Christian mission will continue to find elements of this very mystery hidden in the history and lives, cultures and religions of peoples of diverse faiths. These paschal elements will probably be most evident when seen through life's limit situations of suffering and brokenness. Missioners are continually experiencing the unique ways that the Holy Spirit brings people into direct encounter with the paschal mystery and, yes, with God's salvation in Christ.

The cross of Jesus is the paramount Christian symbol, because it reminds Christians of the centrality of the paschal mystery in their faith lives (Sivalon 381-382). Kosuke Koyama notes: "If Jesus Christ of the cross stands at the center of Christian theology, the Christian Church, the body of Christ, must be called the Church of the cross" (Koyama 1994, 3). All Church missionary activity will focus on the paschal nature of life, of faith, of salvation. Mission is always cruciform, always signed by the cross. *Crux probat omnia.*

Saint Paul spoke of his missionary consciousness in writing to the Corinthian community: "For I decided to know nothing among you except Jesus Christ and him crucified" (I Cor 2:2). To Jews who demanded miracles and Greeks who searched for wisdom, Paul proclaimed a crucified Christ. This message was offensive to the Jews and nonsense to the Gentiles (cf. I Cor 1: 22-25). All the synoptic gospels affirm that the cross is the only path whereby one follows Jesus (Mt 10:38, 16:24; Mk 8:34; Lk 9:23, 14:27). The cross is central to Jesus' act of *kenosis* (Phil 2:5-11); it is pivotal in our salvation from sin (I Pet 2:24).

Pope John Paul II has written: "The mission of the Savior reached its culmination in the Paschal Mystery" (EA 12c). Thus, the cross is not an accidental of Christian faith and mission. As David Bosch writes, the Gospel affirms that "in the suffering Jesus, God embraces the suffering of the world for the sake of humanity.... Moreover, in Christ, God does not necessarily save us *from* suffering, but *in* and *through* it.... Christ suffers when we suffer. The pain people suffer is the pain of Christ himself" (Bosch 585). Christians are called to live into the mystery of the cross, "to live into the image of Christ *on* the cross" (Johns 25). Christian missionary activity must not fail "to keep the cross at the center of salvation and the death of Jesus at the center of the cross" (Frazier 1992, 400).

Roman Catholic missionary communities have a mission-sending ritual during which the new missionaries receive a large crucifix; a cord is attached so it can be worn around the neck. This missionary cross "is no mere ornament depicting Christianity in general. Rather, it is a vigorous commentary on what gives the gospel its universal appeal. Those who receive it possess not only a symbol of their mission, but a handbook on how to carry it out" (Frazier 1987, 44-45). Missionaries who receive the cross in their mission-sending ceremony soon starkly realize that in their direct field experience there is "nothing attractive, easy, secure, comfortable, convenient, strategically efficient, economical, or self-fulfilling about taking up a cross" (Bonk 118).

MISSION AND CONVERSION AS IMPERATIVES. Having noted the reality of suffering in our broken world and having outlined the paschal nature of all reality and of the Christian faith in particular, it is important to state a Christian conviction: mission remains a necessary mandate for the Church in today's world. David Bosch expresses his conviction: "I wish to state unequivocally that I endorse the mission enterprise. I say this because I believe that the Christian faith ... is intrinsically missionary, that the Church—as Vatican II put it—is 'missionary by its very nature'" (Bosch 590).

The document of the World Council of Churches "Mission and Evangelism—An Ecumenical Affirmation" expresses the mission obligation in this manner: "Christians owe the message of God's salvation in Jesus Christ to every person and to every people" (WCC 445). John Paul II affirms "the urgency of missionary evangelization" because "it is the primary service which the Church can render to every individual and to all humanity in the modern world" (RM 2).

The Church is linked to mission and evangelization "in her most intimate being" (EN 15); mission is *not* "an optional contribution for the Church" (EN 5). Quoting Vatican II (AG 29), John Paul II reaffirms that missionary activity is "the greatest and holiest duty of the Church" (RM 63). For Paul VI, the entire Church—and each local Church—realizes her "deepest identity" and "her very nature" when she is in mission (EN 14). She is to be always and everywhere "the universal sacrament of salvation" (LG 48; AG 1). For her, to live is to be missionary!

The Church's mission always bears a Christological focus. *Evangelii Nuntiandi,* the apostolic exhortation of Paul VI, asserts that: "There is no true evangelization if the name, the teaching, the life, the promises, the Kingdom and the mystery of Jesus of Nazareth, the Son of God, are not proclaimed" (EN 22; see EA 19b). This means: "Evangelization will also always contain—as the foundation, center and at the same time summit of its dynamism—a clear proclamation that, in Jesus Christ, the Son of God made man, who died and rose from the dead, salvation is offered to all, as a gift of God's grace and mercy" (EN 27).

A natural corollary of strongly affirming the Church's missionary nature is to affirm the pursuit of conversion through the Christian message she preaches and to which she gives witness. As Church, she "seeks to convert, solely through the divine power of the Message she proclaims" (EN 18). For some persons, conversion as an imperative in Christian mission has slowly gone out of favor. This is unfortunate, because conversion, properly understood, is a necessary part of mission. Conversion has not been detrimental; it has had tremendously beneficial effects on converts (Mondal 13). However, at the same time, it remains crucial to assess the motives, processes, and goals of all conversion; it is crucial to name the conversion process that Christians seek and promote.

NAMING CONVERSION. An impressive body of literature exists on the conversion process; however, totally capturing the nuances and levels of the dynamics of conversion exceeds the scope of this presentation. Many authors use the foundational insights elaborated by Bernard Lonergan who has shown how conversion occurs on various levels (Carroll 1-22; Cronin 19-24; Dulles 1981, 175-185; Gelpi *varia;* Lonergan *varia;* Mueller

13-20; Navone 27-35; Rambo 1993, *varia*). Other authors take a biblical-theological approach to conversion (Beernaert 369-379; Gittins 1993, *varia*; Haqq 84-93; Löffler 24-45; McBrien 7-9; McMahon 56-64). Still others present the psycho-social perspective (Archer 180-190; J. Smith 187-193; P. Smith 62-73). Using selective insights from many sources, this presentation focuses on the *missionary and paschal* dimensions of conversion.

Filled with Christian faith convictions, missionaries seek the conversion of people they encounter. Evangelizers desire that people will shift their horizons, perceive the world in a new way, experience a personal and social transformation. Conversion demands "a radical shift in a person's apprehensions and values, accompanied by a similar radical change in oneself, in one's relations with other persons, and in one's relations to God" (Dulles 1981, 176).

Authentic conversion, in Lonergan's framework, "takes place on four levels related to the four levels of the act of understanding: affective (experience), intellectual (understanding), moral (judging), and religious (deciding). Like the act of understanding, these four conversions are interconnected and dynamically related. To be an integrated person requires a fourfold conversion" (Mueller 16).

Lonergan notes the all-encompassing nature of the conversion process; it is "a transformation of the subject and his world"; it is "a resultant change of course and direction"; it is "existential, intensely personal, utterly intimate." Conversion "affects all of a man's conscious and intentional operations. It directs his gaze, pervades his imagination, releases the symbols that penetrate to the depths of his psyche. It enriches his understanding, guides his judgments, reinforces his decisions" (Lonergan 130-131). Authentic conversion lays total claim to the individual; it "incorporates the totality of our life, because God's love is concerned with that totality" (WCC 433). As Paul wrote to the Ephesians, conversion demands that "Your hearts and minds must be made completely new and you must put on the new self..." (Eph 4:23-24).

Such a total transformation is nothing less than the work of God's grace and the action of the Holy Spirit. It is impossible to "conceive of authentic religious conversion apart from the gracious self-communication of God" (Dulles 1981, 178). All missionaries and evangelizers repeatedly experience the fact that "the Holy Spirit is the principal agent of evangelization (EN 75; cf. RM 21, 30). Mission belongs to God; it is "God's project." Only in the power of the Spirit do mission and conversion progress and bear fruit.

True religious conversion under the action of the Spirit will mean "being grasped by ultimate concern. It is other-worldly falling in love. It is total and permanent self-surrender without conditions, qualifications, reservations" (Lonergan 240). Or, again, it is "unconditional falling in love. It is a love of God with one's whole heart and mind and strength. It is the love of God without restrictions, conditions or reservations. It is moving from a this-worldly horizon to an other-worldly horizon" (Cronin 20). Religious conversion "sets up a new horizon in which the love of God will transvalue our values and the eyes of love will transform our knowing" (Lonergan 106).

The center of this Spirit-inspired conversion and transformation is a loving God; all becomes focused on God's love poured out in the person of Jesus through the paschal mystery. It embraces "the mystery of salvation realized by God for all in Jesus Christ by the power of the Spirit" (DP 10), which is nothing other than the central mystery of Christian faith: the paschal mystery.

The paschal mystery becomes the integrating focus of all mission and conversion. It is foundational because all life has a paschal paradigm—as exemplified in the brokenness of the world in which we live. The "passion of humanity" ever present in wars, famine, oppression, poverty, sickness, hatred, and death is to be the ground in which the seeds of new life, hope, resurrection, and ultimately salvation germinate and bear fruit. This paschal nature of all life and experience (poignantly illustrated by my personal experience with the Bangladeshi beggar-woman) continually provides openings for a deep missionary encounter—and an authentic conversion and transformation into the mystery of God's love.

Recall that illuminating Vatican II quote: "we must hold that the Holy Spirit offers to all the possibility of being made partners, in a way known to God, in the paschal mystery" (GS 22). Thus, every human person— without any exception (RH 14)—has an opportunity to encounter the saving paschal mystery which emerges in and from his or her own life experience which itself has a paschal form. All life, all human experience, all salvation has a paschal character. This is a fundamental human, religious, and Christian insight. All is filled with "paschality." Mission, conversion, and redemption follow this same paschal structure of life.

This is the basic conversion that missionaries and evangelizers seek, the radical transformation desired, the total and permanent self-surrender demanded: unconditional falling in love with God! Human values become transvalued; all is centered on a radical acceptance of the paschal nature of reality. Such a conversion means embracing a broken world and a crucified humanity through the optic of the omnipresent paschal mystery. Christianity seeks a transforming conversion to the paschal view of life. This is the focus of all mission service rendered by the local Churches to humanity in today's peace-starved world.

LEVELS OF MISSIONARY CONVERSION. It has been stated earlier that this presentation focuses on the *missionary and paschal* dimensions of conversion. The experience of field missionaries reveals three interacting levels of conversion into the paschal mystery. The first conversion is centered on the person of the missionary. The second conversion is a call to all persons of faith and good will to embrace a paschal perspective in their lives and consciences. Finally, the third conversion takes the form of an invitation for people to freely join the paschal community of the Christian Church.

Conversion of the Missionary. Christian missionaries begin the conversion process in their own lives and attitudes. They seek to personalize the fact that in the words of John Paul II: "the Church's vocation and missionary commitment spring from the central mystery of our faith: the Paschal Mystery" (WYD 2). They embrace the fact: "The Paschal mystery of Christ's cross and Resurrection stands at the center of the Good News that the apostles, and the Church following them, are to proclaim to the world" (CCC 571).

Evangelizers accept that every missionary begins by entering a personal process of conversion (EN 15). It is true that "the call to conversion should begin with the repentance of those who do the calling, who issue the invitation" (WCC 434). Before crossing any borders of culture or religion to announce the paschal mystery, missionaries seek their own transformation into the same paschal mindset of Jesus (I Cor 2:16; Phil 2:5). Their missionary outlook reflects attitudes of poverty, powerlessness, and vulnerability; they seek personal conversion "according to the image of the serving God in the serving Christ" (Navone 33). To the extent that any missionary embodies the suffering Messiah's self-transcending way of the cross, that person achieves authentic paschal conversion.

It is only with a paschal attitude that the missionary can perceive reality correctly and insightfully. The converted missionary finds in the cross and resurrection of the suffering Messiah the strength and wisdom to address both suffering humanity as well as those who are rushing along the road of individualism, materialism, and consumerism. Paschality becomes the measuring rod for all missionary endeavor, for the life of the local Church.

Conversion to a paschal mentality is a long, continuous, complex process of spiritual growth for every evangelizer. It demands hearing the Gospel repeatedly; it requires renunciation of sin. Conversion "is always a more gradual process than it might seem on the surface" (Schreiter 124); "conversion is a continuous process demanded at every stage of the Christian life ... for no believer has faith fully and securely in hand" (Dulles 1981, 177). Christian life itself is an ongoing conversion, dynamically lived and developing; such an ongoing conversion (and not just a one-time conversion) "is the manner by which we live authentic lives" (Mueller 16). There is no other path to becoming a paschal-centered person ["paschal animal"—Frazier 1992, 400] and to adopting a "crucified mind" rather than a "crusading mind" (Koyama 1974, 117). The individual missionary and the local Church as a missionary community require continual conversion to paschality.

Conversion to a Paschal Worldview. From the paschal perspective operative in the Christian evangelizer's own life, one arrives at a second moment of conversion in the missionary dynamic. Emerging from the common experience of life and death realities, Christian missionaries and all peoples of faith soon recognize the paschal communalities of their shared existence. All peoples—whether Christian, Buddhist or Muslim—share the vicissitudes and challenges of existence in a broken world. All world religions and primal faith systems address with varying degrees of emphasis the mystery of suffering and evil, the reality of wounded humanity (Tesfai 63-66). It is precisely within this shared human existence and mystery that the Christian evangelizer announces paschal perspectives of life through death.

Engaging in a dialogue of life experience, the missionary aims at "deepening the religious experience of all the people involved, at extending the awareness of God's love and human sinfulness, and of motivating everyone involved to eliminate what hinders God's love" (Mantovani 54). The missionary is definitely inviting his or her dialogue partners to a deeper God-experience; this is a spiritual conversion, but not necessarily to Christianity (see DP 11; Burrows 131).

Such a heart-to-heart encounter is a direct effect of the Holy Spirit's action in bringing peoples through their own life situations into a sharing of the paschal mystery. The grace of God is at work everywhere and the fundamental act of faith and conversion is within reach of every human being. The Holy Spirit continually penetrates the concrete lives and histories of people from within and offers them a real mutual participation in the paschal mystery. Yes, for the Christian it will certainly be explicitly Christological. However, the identical experience, although often in an inchoate form, is continually available to all peoples—whatever their particular religious affiliation (see Kroeger 1994, 58).

The missionary calls peoples of all faiths to be converted to this paschal perspective and a concomitant commitment to alleviate the ongoing passion of humankind and the suffering of "crucified peoples" in all times and places. The paschal paradigm "has the power to illumine the truth of the suffering that is omnipresent in creation and history as well as the truth of God in relation to suffering" (Kroeger 1994, 58). At this juncture, it is important to note that the Christian missionary will often find his or her own explicit paschal faith enriched by the implicit paschal faith of his or her Muslim or Buddhist friends.

From a missionary perspective, this presentation has struggled to name the type of conversion sought through efforts of evangelization. It is valid to assert that exemplary missionaries who enable others to embrace a paschal perspective and a selfless servant response to their suffering neighbors have truly accomplished the task of conversion to Gospel values and perspectives. Yes, local Churches have been accomplishing the goal of conversion in several parts of the world, even when, for example in Asia, the number of baptized Christians does not reach three percent!

Christian missionaries through selfless service of the sick, the poor, and victims of injustice have clearly announced the essence of Gospel faith; they have shown the Church to be a caring community of compassion (McCahill 8); they have challenged people to be converted to the paschal mystery and to a deeper love and experience of God. They offer people a paschal perspective in the midst of suffering, challenging them not to become embittered or resentful toward life, people, or even toward God (cf. Sivalon 379-380).

When questioned about the lack of conversions to Christianity in Hindu India, Mother Teresa replied:

"Numbers have nothing to do with it. But the people are putting prayer into action by coming and serving the people. Everywhere people are helping. There may not be a big conversion like that, but we do not know what is happening in the soul.... If people become better Hindus, better Muslims, better Buddhists by our acts of love, then there is something else growing there. They come closer and closer to God. When they come closer, they have to choose" (Kroeger 1990, 105).

Conversion to the Christian Faith Community. All persons are called to conversion which is "the humble and penitent return of the heart to God in the desire to submit one's life more generously to Him" (DM 37). In the course of this process, "the decision may be made to leave one's previous spiritual or religious situation in order to direct oneself towards another" (DM 37). In this conversion process, freedom of conscience is sovereign; "no one must be constrained to act against his conscience, nor ought he to be impeded in acting according to his conscience, especially in religious matters" (DH 3).

Admittedly, mission also has explicit Christian conversion as its goal: "that non-Christians be freely converted to the Lord under the action of the Holy Spirit who opens their hearts so that they may adhere to Him" (AG 13). Christians nourish in their hearts the desire to share their full experience of the paschal mystery and faith in Christ with brothers and sisters of other religions. Missionaries sensitively aim at "guiding people to explicit knowledge of what God has done for all men and women in Jesus Christ, and at inviting them to become disciples of Jesus through becoming members of the Church (DP 81).

One notes the triple dynamic of conversion operative in this missionary process: **(a)** the converted

missionary centers his or her life on the paschal mystery;
(b) the Christian missionary calls other people of faith
to discover the paschal paradigm of life and to adopt
paschal values in their lives, consciences, and service;
(c) based on a free decision inspired by the Spirit, others
are directly invited to join the community of the Christian
Church, where they can fully practice their paschal-
mystery-centered faith.

The paschal nature of life, faith, and redemption
integrates the entire conversion process. Awareness of
and participation in the paschal mystery often unfold in
the lives of people in an evolutionary and progressive
manner. The evangelizer finds the paschal mystery
operative and recognizes conversion both outside and
within the Church. Affirming the action of the Spirit
beyond the borders of the Church "does not cancel the
need for having a community of the disciples, the Church,
that has experienced the all-inclusive love of the Father
in Jesus and commits itself to continue his mission"
(Kavunkal 187). This wide, inclusive view of mission and
the workings of the Holy Spirit adds further meaning to
the reality of the missionary local Church as the "universal
sacrament of salvation" (LG 48; AG 1).

ADDITIONAL MISSION COROLLARIES. This
presentation has strongly affirmed the validity of
centering mission and conversion within the framework
of the paschal mystery. It is a "paschal missiology" and
challenges all missionaries to become "paschal
evangelizers" in their own lives and through their
approaches to the Church's missionary activity. In the
context of today's broken world, the enormous afflictions
and sufferings of humanity, and the need to maintain
eschatological hope, paschal missiology appears
particularly insightful, necessary, and relevant.

In this concluding section of this presentation,
other missiological themes and their intimate

relationship to paschal mission approaches are noted. The insights, flowing from a paschal-mystery-centered missiology, are numerous; these "corollaries" are only mentioned very briefly (a full elaboration exceeds the scope of this presentation); their relationship to paschal mission perspectives is also highlighted.

(1) Paschal mission emerges from the unity of all humanity in its sharing of the common paschal experience of rising through dying. All peoples face questions of suffering as well as the mystery and meaning of life.

(2) Paschal mission uses an inductive approach based on experience to understand the Church's call to mission. Each local Church is called to be active in "reading the signs of the times and of interpreting them in the light of the Gospel" (GS 4); human suffering and brokenness constitute a missionary challenge today.

(3) Paschal mission strongly affirms the active presence of the Holy Spirit in the world, both in and beyond the boundaries of the Church. The Spirit is constantly directing people to a God-encounter through their sharing in the paschal mystery.

(4) Paschal mission embodies the virtue of Christian hope based on the firm belief in the resurrection. Eschatological hope, not suffering, is the integrating perspective of Christian mission; that hope continually breaks into the world through missionary witness and service.

(5) Paschal mission clearly allows missioners to be people of integrity. Their proclamation begins with their own paschal experiences and links them with people who share identical experiences. Mission is not something superimposed upon reality; mission emerges from the commonly shared realities of missioners and their dialogue partners of various faiths.

(6) Paschal mission demands a radical conversion of the missioner to the values of a crucified-risen Lord; mission begins only when personal transformation has been initiated. Only the converted missioner can authentically call others to conversion.

(7) Paschal mission requires the integration of contemplation into missionary praxis. No one can authentically address the "passion of humanity" without possessing a deep contemplative faith; one must live into the paschal mystery.

(8) Paschal mission emphasizes that the work of the missionary involves both listening and speaking. Listening for the Spirit's action within the hearts and lives of people is a prerequisite for speaking of God's paschal love and saving deeds.

(9) Paschal mission lays bare the sinfulness of today's world which is so often enslaved in materialism, consumerism, individualism, greed, and pride. A paschal mentality challenges both personal and social sin; it demands true conversion.

(10) Paschal mission respects the free will and personal conscience of everyone; at the same time it is a call to conscience for generous people (Christians and non-Christians alike) to be committed to addressing the sufferings of humanity.

(11) Paschal mission easily enters into dialogue with the followers of other religions. All religious traditions face identical human questions and mysteries. Dialogue enables peoples of faith to mutually explore and respond to questions of life and death.

(12) Paschal mission connects intimately with today's challenges of peace, justice, development, and ecology. It invites all to live in solidarity with their neighbors and to be prepared to suffer and die so that others may live. Again, such a paschal life-style demands profound conversion.

(13) Paschal mission can be lived in all cultural contexts and situations. As a missionary approach it easily finds an inculturated home among diverse peoples. Paschal mission is also clearly transcultural.

(14) Paschal mission aims to be a holistic approach to mission, integrating the personal and social, the human and divine, the material and spiritual. It is an incarnational approach to being in mission.

(15) Paschal mission emphasizes humble and self-effacing approaches to missionary activity; it consciously seeks to avoid any pitfalls of paternalism or colonialism. Missioners, believing in the beauty and truth of their message, seek to offer it with generosity, sincerity, and authenticity.

(16) Paschal mission is at heart a scripture-based missiology. It follows the teachings and example of Jesus who came "not to be served but to serve, and to give his life as a ransom for many" (Mt 20:28).

(17) Paschal mission embodies an emphasis on witness and even a willingness to endure suffering, persecution, and martyrdom. Contemporary missionaries knowingly and willingly embrace vulnerability, because in Christ God reveals himself precisely in weakness rather than in power.

(18) Paschal mission is at heart a soteriology. Following the paschal path in mission brings both evangelizer and people into a direct experience of salvation in Jesus Christ, who "bore our sins in his own body on the cross; ... through his wounds [we] have been healed" (I Pet 2:24).

(19) Paschal mission integrates well with the sacramental dimension of the Church. All Christians are missionary by virtue of their baptism into Christ's death and resurrection (Rom 6:3-4). The Eucharist is the paschal meal that celebrates the death and resurrection of the Lord until He comes (I Cor 11:23-26); the Eucharist remains the "ongoing sacrament of mission" for Christians.

(20) Paschal mission transforms the individual missioner into an attractive and credible witness. Missioners of the caliber of a Mother Teresa manifest the transforming effects of the paschal mystery in their lives, and today's world welcomes such authentic witnesses, icons of paschal faith and service.

CONCLUDING REFLECTION. This presentation began with a narration of an encounter between a missionary and a Bangladeshi beggar-woman. That "defining experience" has produced much depth reflection on the nature of mission and conversion. This missionary remains filled with gratitude for that God-given experience of grace. More reflection needs to be given to the wealth of insights that can still emerge from viewing mission through the optic of the paschal mystery. And finally, relying on God's grace, this missionary looks forward to meeting that Muslim Bangladeshi beggar-woman once again in the resurrected life with Christ the Lord in heaven. I am confident she will be there!

ABBREVIATIONS: CHURCH DOCUMENTS

AG   - *Ad Gentes* (Missionary Activity: December 7, 1965)

DH   - *Dignitatis Humanae* (Religious Liberty: December 7, 1965)

DM   - *Dialogue and Mission* (Pontifical Council for Interreligious Dialogue: June 10, 1984)

DP   - *Dialogue and Proclamation* (Pontifical Council for Interreligious Dialogue: May 19, 1991)

EA   - *Ecclesia in Asia* (The Church in Asia: November 6, 1999)

EN   - *Evangelii Nuntiandi* (Evangelization in the Modern World: December 8, 1975)

GS   - *Gaudium et Spes* (The Church in the Modern World: December 7, 1965)

LG   - *Lumen Gentium* (The Church: November 21, 1964)

LR   - *La Realta* (The Reality of Suffering / John Paul II: April 27, 1994)

RH   - *Redemptor Hominis* (Mystery of Redemption and Human Dignity: March 4, 1979)

RM   - *Redemptoris Missio* (The Mission of the Redeemer: December 7, 1990)

SD   - *Salvifici Dolores* (The Christian Meaning of Human Suffering / John Paul II: February 11, 1984)

WYD - *World Youth Days IX and X Message* (John Paul II: November 21, 1993)

SELECTED BIBLIOGRAPHY

CONVERSION AND THE PASCHAL MYSTERY

Archer, A. "Theology and Sociology: Two Approaches to Religious Conversion." *New Blackfriars* 62/730 (April, 1981): 180-190.

Beernaert, P. "Converting to the Gospel." *Lumen Vitae* 42/4 (1987): 369-379.

Bonk, J. *Missions and Money.* Maryknoll, New York: Orbis Books, 1991.

Bosch, D. "The Vulnerability of Mission." *Vidyajyoti* 56/11 (November, 1992): 577-596.

Burrows, W., ed. *Redemption and Dialogue: Reading Redemptoris Missio and Dialogue and Proclamation.* Maryknoll, New York: Orbis Books, 1994.

Carroll, M. *Framework for a Theology of Christian Conversion in the Jesus-Project of Edward Schillebeeckx.* Washington: The Catholic University of America, 1984.

Catechism of the Catholic Church (CCC). Liguori, Missouri: Liguori Publications, 1994.

Cronin, B. "Religious and Christian Conversion in an African Context." *African Christian Studies* 3/2 (June, 1987): 9-35.

Dulles, A. **[A]** "Fundamental Theology and the Dynamics of Conversion." *Thomist* 45/2 (April, 1981): 175-193. **[B]** "Conversion." In *Dictionary of Fundamental Theology,* ed. R. Latourelle and R. Fisichella, 191-193. New York: The Crossroad Publishing Company, 1994.

Fernando, A. *Buddhism Made Plain*. Maryknoll, New York: Orbis Books, 1990.

Francis, M. *"Why the Innocent Suffer?* Hyderabad, India: Saint John's Regional Seminary, 1998.

Frazier, W. **[A]** "Where Mission Begins: A Foundational Probe." *Maryknoll Formation Journal* 6/2 (1987): 13-50. **[B]** "The Incredible Christian Capacity for Missing the Christian Point." *America* 167/16 (November 21, 1992): 398-400.

Gelpi, D. *The Conversion Experience*. New York: Paulist Press, 1998.

Gittins, A. **[A]** *Bread for the Journey*. Maryknoll, New York: Orbis Books, 1993. **[B]** "Conversion." In *Dictionary of Mission: Theology, History, Perspectives*, ed. K. Müller et al., 87-89. Maryknoll, New York: Orbis Books, 1997.

Haqq, A. "Conversion." *The Bulletin of Christian Institutes of Islamic Studies* 6/3-4 (1983): 75-93.

John Paul II. **[A]** *"Salvifici Doloris* - The Christian Meaning of Human Suffering [February 11, 1984]." *The Pope Speaks* 29/2 (1985): 105-139. **[B]** *"La Realta* - The Lord Sanctifies Those Who Suffer [April 27, 1994]." *The Pope Speaks* 39/5 (1994): 316-318.

Johns, E. "A Journey Into Spiritual Community." *America* 171/12 (October 22, 1994): 24-26.

Kavunkal, J. "Dialogue and Conversion." *Vidyajyoti* 54/4 (April, 1990): 177-187.

Koyama, K. **[A]** "What Makes a Missionary? Toward Crucified Mind, Not Crusading Mind." In *Mission Trends No. 1.* ed. G. Anderson and T. Stransky, 117-132. New York: Paulist Press, 1974. **[B]** "The Theology of the Cross and the Self-Consciousness of the Church." *Asia Journal of Theology* 8/1 (April, 1994): 2-12.

Kroeger, J. **[A]** *Interreligious Dialogue. Catholic Perspectives.* Davao City, Philippines: Mission Studies Institute, 1990. **[B]** *Living Mission: Challenges in Evangelization Today.* Maryknoll, New York: Orbis Books and Quezon City, Philippines: Claretian Publications, 1994. **[C]** "Bridging Interreligious Dialogue and Conversion." *Review for Religious* 55/1 (January-February, 1996): 46-54.

Löffler, P. "The Biblical Concept of Conversion." In *Mission Trends No. 2.* ed. G. Anderson and T. Stransky, 24-45. New York: Paulist Press, 1975.

Lonergan, B. *Method in Theology.* New York: Herder and Herder, 1972.

Mantovani, E. "Dialogue with Primal Religions." In *Mission and Dialogue.* ed. L. Mercado and J. Knight, 48-60. Manila: Divine Word Publications, 1989.

Martin, D. "Individual and Collective Conversion of Hearts." *L'Osservatore Romano* 34/37 (September 12, 2001): 7.

McBrien, R. "Models of Conversion: An Ecclesiological Reflection." *Living Light* 18/1 (Spring, 1981): 7-17.

McCahill, R. "Conversion Is Not the Purpose, Building Trust Is." *Asia Focus* 10/16 (May 6, 1994): 8.

McMahon, C. "Call, Conversion, and Catechesis in St. Paul." *Living Light* 37/4 (Summer, 2001): 56-64.

Moling, A. "The Paschal Mystery and Non-Christian Religions and Cultures." *Bulletin: Secretariatus pro Non Christianis* 21/3 [63] (1986): 288-295.

Mondal, A. "Place of Conversion in Christian Mission." *Mission Outlook* (1993): 12-14.

Mueller, S. *What Are They Saying about Theological Method?* New York: Paulist Press, 1984.

Mussner, F. "Should We Still Seek Converts?" *Theology Digest* 24/2 (Summer, 1976): 132-136.

Navone, J. "Four Complementary Dimensions of Conversion." *Studies in Formative Spirituality* 10/1 (February, 1989): 27-35.

Oommen, G. "Conversion in India: A Historical Appraisal with Reference to M.K. Gandhi's Response to Conversion." *Bangalore Theological Forum* 32/1 (June, 2000): 154-164.

PCID (Pontifical Council for Interreligious Dialogue). **[A]** "The Attitude of the Church Towards the Followers of Other Religions: Reflections and Orientations on Mission and Dialogue." *L'Osservatore Romano* 17/26 (June 25, 1984): 10-11. **[B]** "Dialogue and Proclamation: Reflections and Orientations on Interreligious Dialogue and the Proclamation of the Gospel of Jesus Christ." Vatican City: PCID, 1991.

Peiró, J. "El Budismo y el enigma de la existencia sufriente." *Razon y Fe* 229/1,146 (1994): 403-414.

Rahner, K. "Conversion." In *Sacramentum Mundi* II, 4-8. New York: Herder and Herder, 1968.

Rambo, L. **[A]** "Conversion." In *The Encyclopedia of Religion* - IV, ed. M. Eliade, 73-79. New York: Macmillan Publishing Company, 1987. **[B]** *Understanding Religious Conversion.* New Haven, Connecticut: Yale University Press, 1993.

Richard, L. *What Are They Saying About the Theology of Suffering?* New York: Paulist Press, 1992.

Schreiter, R. "Changes in Roman Catholic Attitudes toward Proselytism and Mission." In *New Directions in*

Mission and Evangelization II, ed. J. Scherer and S. Bevans, 113-125. Maryknoll, New York: Orbis Books, 1994.

Sivalon, J. "Mission and Suffering of the Innocent." *Missiology* 30/3 (July, 2002): 375-383.

Smith, J. "The Human Character of Conversion." *Journal of Spiritual Formation* 15/2 (1994): 187-193.

Smith, P. "Conversion à la James: Some Contemporary Applications." *The American Benedictine Review* 45/1 (March, 1994): 62-73.

Sobrino, J. *The Principle of Mercy.* Maryknoll, New York: Orbis Books, 1994.

Tesfai, Y. *The Scandal of a Crucified World.* Maryknoll, New York: Orbis Books, 1994.

Witherup, R. *Conversion in the New Testament.* Collegeville, Minnesota: The Liturgical Press, 1994.

World Council of Churches (WCC). "Mission and Evangelism—An Ecumenical Affirmation." *International Review of Mission* 71/284 (October, 1982): 427-451.

BOOKS BY JAMES H. KROEGER

THE FUTURE OF THE ASIAN CHURCHES:
  THE ASIAN SYNOD AND ECCLESIA IN ASIA.
    Quezon City, Philippines: Claretian Publications, 2002.

SONS OF SAN JOSE: THE JOSEFINO SPIRIT—A PROFILE.
    Quezon City, Philippines: San Jose Seminary Alumni Association, 2002.

TELLING GOD'S STORY: NATIONAL MISSION CONGRESS 2000.
    Quezon City, Philippines: Claretian Publications, 2001.

LANDAS JUBILEE 2000.
    Quezon City, Philippines: Loyola School of Theology, 2001.

TELL THE WORLD: CATECHETICAL MODULES FOR MISSION ANIMATION.
    Quezon City, Philippines: Claretian Publications, 2000.

ASIA-CHURCH IN MISSION.
    Quezon City, Philippines: Claretian Publications, 1999.

LIVING MISSION IN ASIA.
    Hong Kong: Federation of Asian Bishops' Conferences, 1999.

REMEMBERING OUR BISHOP JOSEPH W. REGAN, M.M.
    Quezon City, Philippines: Claretian Publications, 1998.

CONTEMPORARY MISSION ISSUES.
   A Series of eleven pamphlets on Mission Issues.
   Maryknoll, New York: Maryknoll Press, 1995-1997.

LIVING MISSION: CHALLENGES IN EVANGELIZATION TODAY.
   Maryknoll, New York: Orbis Books, 1994.
   Quezon City, Philippines: Claretian Publications, 1994.

MISSION TODAY: CONTEMPORARY THEMES IN MISSIOLOGY.
   Hong Kong: Federation of Asian Bishops' Conferences, 1991.

INTERRELIGIOUS DIALOGUE: CATHOLIC PERSPECTIVES.
   Davao City, Philippines: Mission Studies Institute, 1990.

KNOWING CHRIST JESUS: A CHRISTOLOGICAL SOURCEBOOK.
   Quezon City, Philippines: Claretian Publications, 1989.

CHURCH TRULY ALIVE: JOURNEY TO THE FILIPINO REVOLUTION.
   Davao City, Philippines: Mission Studies Institute, 1988.

ADVANCED CEBUANO COLLOQUIAL EXPRESSSIONS
   Davao City, Philippines: Institute of Language and Culture, 1986.

THE PHILIPPINE CHURCH AND EVANGELIZATION: 1965-1984.
   Rome, Italy: Gregorian University Press, 1985.

* * *

JAMES H. KROEGER, Maryknoll Missioner, is Professor of Systematic Theology, Missiology, and Islamics at the Loyola School of Theology, Ateneo de Manila University, Philippines. He holds Licentiate and Doctorate Degrees in Missiology from the Pontifical Gregorian University, Rome. Kroeger has served mission in Asia (Philippines and Bangladesh) since 1970. He is also President of the Philippine Association of Catholic Missiologists (PACM), Secretary-Convenor of the Asian Missionary Societies Forum (AMSAL), and consultant to the Asian Bishops' (FABC) Office of Evangelization.